Notes *on* Nuance

Volume 1

Patrick Barry

Copyright © 2020 by Patrick Barry
Some rights reserved

This work is licensed under the Creative Commons Attribution-NonCommercial-NoDerivatives 4.0 International License. To view a copy of this license, visit http://creativecommons.org/licenses/by-nc-nd/4.0/ or send a letter to Creative Commons, PO Box 1866, Mountain View, California, 94042, USA.

Published in the United States of America by
Michigan Publishing
Manufactured in the United States of America

DOI: http://dx.doi.org/10.3998/mpub.11678299

ISBN 978-1-60785-610-8 (paper)
ISBN 978-1-60785-611-5 (e-book)
ISBN 978-1-60785-612-2 (OA)

An imprint of Michigan Publishing, Maize Books serves the publishing needs of the University of Michigan community by making high-quality scholarship widely available in print and online. It represents a new model for authors seeking to share their work within and beyond the academy, offering streamlined selection, production, and distribution processes. Maize Books is intended as a complement to more formal modes of publication in a wide range of disciplinary areas.
http://www.maizebooks.org

For my sister Christine, whose thoughtful style and overall approach to life is its own form of nuance

Here, she found, everything had nuance; everything had an unrevealed side or unexplored depths.

—Celeste Ng, *Little Fires Everywhere* (2017)

CONTENTS

Introduction — 1
　Future Versions — 3
　Structure — 4

Chapter 1: "Un-" — 7
　Overview — 8
　Notes — 9
　Practice — 11

Chapter 2: "Almost" and "Even" — 15
　Overview — 16
　Notes — 17
　Practice — 21

Chapter 3: Chiasmus ("A-B-B-A") — 25
　Overview — 26
　Notes — 28
　Practice — 31

Chapter 4: "If"—"If"—"If Not" — 33
　Overview — 34
　Notes — 35
　Practice — 37
　Review — 39

CONTENTS

Chapter 5: "As" — 41
    Overview — 42
    Notes — 43
    Practice — 45

Chapter 6: Nuance Spotlight (Jane Austen) — 49
    Overview — 50
    Notes — 51

Chapter 7: "At Once" — 53
    Overview — 54
    Notes — 55
    Practice — 58

Chapter 8: "Equal Parts" — 61
    Overview — 62
    Notes — 63
    Practice — 65
    Review — 67

Chapter 9: "To" — 69
    Overview — 70
    Notes — 72
    Practice — 75

Chapter 10: "Albeit" — 77
    Overview — 78
    Notes — 80
    Practice — 82

Chapter 11: "However" — 85
    Overview — 86
    Notes — 88
    Practice — 91

CONTENTS

Chapter 12: "At Best, At Worst" — 95
  Overview — 96
  Notes — 99
  Practice — 101

Chapter 13: Nuance Spotlight (James Baldwin) — 103
  Overview — 104
  Notes — 106

Chapter 14: "What ____ Is To ____" — 107
  Overview — 108
  Notes — 109
  Practice — 111

Chapter 15: "Let Alone" and "Much Less" — 115
  Overview — 116
  Notes — 118
  Practice — 121

Chapter 16: "As Diverse As" — 123
  Overview — 124
  Notes — 126
  Practice — 128
  Review — 130

Chapter 17: "More ____ Than ____" — 133
  Overview — 134
  Notes — 135
  Practice — 138

Chapter 18: "Less ____ Than ____" and "Less Than" — 141
  Overview — 142
  Notes — 144
  Practice: "Less ___ Than ___" — 146
  Practice: "Less Than ___" — 148

CONTENTS

Chapter 19: Nuance Spotlight (William F. Buckley Jr.) — 149
    Overview — 150
    Notes — 152

Chapter 20: "Without Being" and "Without" — 155
    Overview — 156
    Notes — 158
    Practice — 160

Chapter 21: "All But" — 163
    Overview — 164
    Notes — 165
    Practice — 168
    Review — 170

Chapter 22: "Where" — 171
    Overview — 172
    Notes — 175
    Practice — 178
    Review — 180

Chapter 23: "But Not" — 181
    Overview — 182
    Notes — 184
    Practice — 186
    Review — 188

Chapter 24: Nuance Spotlight (*The Economist*) — 191
    Overview — 192
    Notes — 194

Chapter 25: Double Moves — 197
    Overview — 198

Answer Key — 201
Photo Credits — 211
Notes — 215
Acknowledgments — 243

INTRODUCTION

Notes on Nuance is designed to reveal the hidden mechanics that skilled writers use to add style and sophistication to their sentences and slogans. I originally created the content as a subsection of *Good with Words: Writing and Editing*, a book that came out in the spring of 2019 and has now been turned into an online course with the help of the digital learning platform Coursera. But the student reactions to the *Notes on Nuance* material in classes I have taught at both the University of Michigan Law School and the University of Chicago Law School have been so positive that I decided to turn it into its own project. As one student wrote on a course feedback form, "The *Notes on Nuance* exercises are fantastic. I've actively worked to apply them to my writing and have included several already. Keep making them." Others added that the exercises are "super interesting" and "really helpful in exposing me to new styles of writing and pushing me to think in a different way about sentences." I hope you'll have a similar experience.

I also hope you realize you don't have to be a law student or lawyer to benefit from the lessons this book contains. One of the best parts of my job is that students from other disciplines often sign up for my courses and workshops. Here's a sample of represented programs from a recent semester.

- Business
- Economics
- Health Informatics
- Public Health
- Public Policy
- School of Art and Design
- School of Education
- School of Engineering
- School of Information
- School of Nursing
- School of Social Work

To succeed in any of these fields, it is becoming increasingly important to distinguish yourself as a savvy communicator. Social media has only accelerated the ways in which we all must learn to use our words to connect, compete, and create—sometimes all at once. There are features of the English language, however, that many of us haven't taken full advantage of yet. *Notes on Nuance* is designed to help change that.

Its target audience is that substantial portion of people (myself included) for whom a little extra writerly refinement could make a major difference, whether in school, at work, or simply through personal correspondences.

Unlike many style guides, however, this one is not going to focus on rhetorical terms such as "anaphora," "epistrophe," and "anadiplosis." These terms can be great for certain students, and I recommend Ward Farnsworth's excellent compendium *Classical English Rhetoric* to anyone looking to learn a whole suite of them. But I haven't had a ton of success getting the technical names for writing techniques to resonate with the folks who take my classes. It can be tough to even pronounce "anadiplosis," much less remember how to use it.

INTRODUCTION

Notes on Nuance differs in another way from other style guides, many of which are filled with a rather homogenous set of mostly white—and often long-dead—exemplars. I have nothing against trying to learn from the expertly crafted words of Winston Churchill, Charles Dickens, George Eliot, and Jane Austen. You'll find sentences from each of them in the chapters that follow. But you'll also find a much more deliberately diverse collection of models. Among them are Zadie Smith, Atul Gawande, Salman Rushdie, Gish Jen, Angela Duckworth, Ta-Nehisi Coates, Gabriel García Márquez, Jhumpa Lahiri, Octavia Butler, Mohsin Hamid, and Haruki Murakami. Nuanced writing is, in my view, inclusive writing. And given that my students aren't all white men and women, I don't think the materials they learn to write with should be either.

Future Versions

The diversity of sources included in *Notes on Nuance* highlights something encouraging: doctors can write with nuance; journalists can write with nuance; psychologists and historians and physicists can write with nuance; pretty much anyone can write with nuance, provided they learn the right rhetorical moves.

The way I have organized these moves over the past several years has been twofold. First, I have organized them by move. Each technique you'll learn about has an individual file. Second, I have organized them by subject, the major ones being law, business, sports, science, politics, medicine, movies, television, music, and kids. When I use the materials in class, I combine all the subjects together. The law students and graduate students I teach come from a broad spectrum of college majors: statistics, history, chemistry, sociology, physics, anthropology, math, urban planning, music, and many more. So I try to make the examples they learn from similarly wide-ranging.

The helpful consequence of this approach is that I now have (1) a central collection of *Notes on Nuance* that has been class-tested on a pool of heterogeneous readers and (2) plenty of content with which to create much more specialized companion collections. The book you are reading is drawn from the central collection. But perhaps at some point it might be nice to produce something like *Notes on Nuance: Science*, or *Notes on Nuance: Sports*, or *Notes on Nuance: The Supreme Court*.

I am not sure each of these *Notes on Nuance* companions warrants its own volume. But one of the things that really excites me about the project is the chance to adapt and expand it, particularly online. For updates on that, visit "Good Sentences" (https://libguides.law.umich.edu/goodsentences), a digital library at the University of Michigan Law School created with the idea that to write good sentences, you need to read good sentences.

Structure: Nuance Spotlight, Nuance Practice, Nuance Review

Most of the chapters in this book include examples from an eclectic assortment of writers. But there are also several "Nuance Spotlight" chapters that give you a chance to see how a few especially accomplished wordsmiths use the nuance moves we'll be examining. These include Jane Austen, James Baldwin, William F. Buckley Jr., and the cleverly concise journalists at *The Economist*. Studying how individual stylists put together sentences is a good way to upgrade how you assemble your own.

Perhaps the most useful pages of the book, however, come at the end of each chapter. There you'll get to practice and review what you've learned. UCLA psychologist Robert Bjork and many others have amassed a lot of evidence showing that just reading material isn't nearly as effective as testing yourself and creating what he calls

INTRODUCTION

"desirable difficulty." The "Nuance Practice" and "Nuance Review" exercises provide the opportunity to do that. They're designed to help you move beyond just superficially recognizing content. The best, longest-lasting benefits come from effortful retrieval. Knowledge deepens when we have to work a bit to store and recall it.*

An even better approach, of course, is to start experimenting with these nuance moves in your own writing. Try them in a text message. Insert a couple into an informal email or tweet. Then, once you get more comfortable, use them to enliven and diversify your more high-stakes writing as well.

I'm not suggesting that you put them in every sentence you write. A key part of nuance is restraint. But if you never experiment with these moves, much of their value will be wasted. They are not museum pieces. Just the opposite, in fact: they respond well to frequent and courageous use. So take them out into the world. Incorporate them into your paragraphs and projects. See what they can do for you at work, in school, or wherever else being good with words matters.

You'll likely botch your initial attempts. That's okay. Nuance isn't a skill you can instantly download. I hope, however, you'll also discover that by focusing on the mechanics of expression, by developing new ways to *frame* your ideas, you can increase your *range* of ideas—and with any luck, the quality of them as well. Said differently, structure, when thoughtfully considered, can both generate content and improve it.

---

* If you find the exercises unhelpful or tiresome, however, feel free to skip them. I can definitely understand wanting to read a book without having to do what might feel like homework.

ONE

"Un-"

*He went back to America <u>unslaved</u>.
<u>Unslaved</u>. It was a curious and lovely word,
and I liked Manyaki all the more for it.*

—Colum McCann, *TransAtlantic* (2013)

*"I've had a lot of experience with the
justice system," Sharif said.
"It's all about <u>un-law</u> and <u>un-care</u>."*

—Karan Mahajan, *The Association of Small Bombs* (2016)

Overview

When you attach the prefix "un-" to a word that normally stands alone, you can create a clever reorientation. A good example comes in a work of fiction that John Updike selected as one of the best short stories of the twentieth century: "Birthmates" by Gish Jen. The story focuses on Art Woo, a not-very-successful salesperson whose marriage has recently ended. Jen uses a well-placed *un-* to frame how Art assesses the likelihood he and his wife will reconcile. "Sometimes people get <u>un</u>divorced," Art says, "but you can't exactly count on it."

Jen could have had Art say something more conventional. She could have had him say, "Sometimes people <u>remarry</u> each other" or "Sometimes people <u>get back together</u>." But instead she used this *un-* move, inserting a subtle shift in language and perspective: "Sometimes people get <u>un</u>divorced."

Ta-Nehisi Coates, the best-selling author of *Between the World and Me* and *The Water Dancer*, does something similar in a 2015 essay on mass incarceration. "For African Americans," he explains, "<u>un</u>freedom is the historical norm." Like the word "divorce," the word "freedom" is not typically preceded by *un-*. The *un-* in terms like "unforgettable" or "unexpected" is pretty familiar—to the point where we might not even notice it. But the *un-* in "unfreedom" pops off the page. It's an attention-grabber, the kind of construction that signals that the author is keenly aware of what words can do.

The Notes section that follows includes additional examples, as does the Practice section, where a series of short questions gives you the opportunity to practice how to use the move yourself.

Notes

1. **Note how one "un-" sometimes attracts another.**
   "Now it is admitted that the deliberate killing of this <u>unoffending</u> and <u>unresisting</u> boy was clearly murder, unless the killing can be justified by some well-recognized excuse admitted by the law."
   —Lord Coleridge, *Regina v. Dudley & Stephens* (1884)

   "The growing good of the world is partly dependent on <u>unhistoric</u> acts; and that things are not so ill with you and me as they might have been, is half owing to the number who lived faithfully a hidden life, and rest in <u>unvisited</u> tombs."
   —George Eliot, *Middlemarch* (1871)

2. **Note how companies sometimes use "un-" to promote their products.**
   7Up: "The Uncola"
   T-Mobile: "The Un-Carrier"
   Jimmy John's Gourmet Sandwiches: "The Unwich"
   Labatt Beer: "Get Undomesticated"

3. **Note how putting "not" before your "un-" word creates a double negative that can then be used to assert something like a positive statement. (These combinations are often called "litotes.")**
   "Slim and compact and <u>not unhandsome</u> in his dark suit, he was small—by the time Cecilia was thirteen, both his women overtopped him—with a neatly trimmed beard and brown eyes that were unexpectedly limpid and expressive, suggesting that he held back strong feeling."
   —Tessa Hadley, "Cecilia Awakened" (2018)

"There were certain things in life that Bill would go to almost any length to avoid, and one was going to a barbershop. The very idea of the physical intimacy inherent to the hair-cutting process overwhelmed him, and from the time that I had met him in California, he had sported long, glossy black hair that was <u>not unreminiscent</u> of Cher's."
—Hope Jahren, *Lab Girl* (2016)

"But when the feasting was over, the villagers told themselves that they had underrated the power of the ballot paper before and should not do so again. Chief the Honorable Marcus Ibe was <u>not unprepared</u>. He had drawn five months' salary in advance, changed a few hundred pounds into shining shillings and armed his campaign boys with eloquent little jute bags."
—Chinua Achebe, "The Voter" (1965)

4. **Note how not everyone is a fan of using "un-" this way.**

"One can cure oneself of the *not un-* formation by memorizing this sentence: *A <u>not unblack</u> dog was chasing a <u>not unsmall</u> rabbit across a <u>not ungreen</u> field.*"
—George Orwell, "Politics and the English Language" (1946)

"UN-"

Nuance Practice*

(1) William Finnegan won a Pulitzer Prize for his 2015 memoir *Barbarian Days: A Surfing Life*. In the following sentences, he describes his first day surfing in Hawaii.

> The surfers were good. They all had smooth, _____ styles. Nobody fell off. And nobody, blessedly, seemed to notice me.

Pick the missing "un-" word.

(A) unsmelly
(B) ungimmicky
(C) unencumbered
(D) unintentional

(2) The review of Finnegan's book in *Sports Illustrated* made the following comparison: "Reading this guy on the subject of waves and water is like reading Hemingway on bullfighting." Hemingway, incidentally, also used the *un-* move, in a 1936 short story called "The Capital of the World."

> He was a well built boy with black, rather curly hair, good teeth and a skin that his sisters envied, and he had a ready and _____ smile.

(A) unprepossessing
(B) unpuzzled
(C) unperturbed
(D) unexpected

---

* For answers, see page 201 of the Answer Key.

(3) On what twentieth-century author's gravestone is written the following: "Death is the enemy. Against you I will fling myself, <u>unvanquished</u> and <u>unyielding</u>, O Death! The waves broke on the shore."?

    (A) Emily Brontë
    (B) Emily Dickinson
    (C) Virginia Woolf
    (D) Amy Tan

<u>Hint</u>: Nicole Kidman won an Oscar for playing her in the 2002 film *The Hours*.

(4) In David Gilbert's 2017 short story "The Sightseers," a city dweller named Robert marvels at the space and greenness of another character's backyard.

> As they talked, Robert strolled through the expansive back yard, his eyes taking in the trees and the boxwoods and the wondrous grass, the absolute _____ aspect of this sanctuary, but also appreciating the bluestone paths and terrace.

    (A) unrural
    (B) unidyllic
    (C) un-Montana
    (D) un-Manhattan

(5) James Shapiro is a professor of English at Columbia University and a governor of the Folger Shakespeare Library. Which Shakespearean tragedy is he describing when he writes the following?

> The negativity is reinforced by the sixty or so times the prefix "un" occurs, as characters are "unfriended," "unprized," "unfortunate," "unmannerly," "unnatural," and "unmerciful." Call it what you will—resistance, refusal, denial, rejection, repudiation—this insistent and almost apocalyptic negativity becomes a recurring drumbeat, the bass line of the play.

Answer: K _ n _
    L _ a _

TWO

"Almost" and "Even"

When I turned on the landing of the Lyceum stairs, I was shocked to see him sitting in the windowsill. I glanced at him quickly, and then quickly away, and was about to walk into the hall when he said, "Wait." His voice was cool and Bostonian, <u>almost</u> British.

—Donna Tartt, *The Secret History* (1992)

Snoopy had his origins in Spike, the dog of Schulz's youth, whom Sparky called "the wildest and the smartest dog I've ever encountered," and as long as Snoopy was treated as a pet—an eccentric, <u>even</u> a lunatic, household dog—by the Peanuts *gang, he evinced Spike-like behavior.*

—David Michaelis, *Schulz and Peanuts: A Biography* (2007)

Overview

The nuance move we are going to learn in this chapter involves two words: *almost* and *even*. We'll see that each can help you gesture toward a more extreme word without fully committing to it. Consider, for example, the following sentence from the novel *Lolita* by Vladimir Nabokov.

> Gently I rolled back to town, in that old faithful car of mine which was serenely, <u>almost</u> cheerfully working for me.

See how Nabokov gestures toward the word "cheerfully" without fully committing to it? The old faithful car of his was *almost* cheerfully working for him, but Nabokov isn't prepared to say it was *actually* cheerfully working for him. He's not ready to bump his description of the car to that extra level. So after the word *serenely*, he slides in the word *almost*, which creates a stylish way of communicating subtle gradations.

You can do something similar with the word *even*, as the next example shows. It comes from the novel *The Round House* by Louise Erdrich.

> I'm okay, she said through the Kleenex. Her voice sounded normal, <u>even</u> detached.

There are a number of variations of both *almost* and *even* in the Notes section of this chapter. You'll see that some writers choose to punctuate these moves with commas, while others prefer dashes. Experiment with both options, in a trial-and-error kind of way. Nuance isn't an innate, inheritable characteristic. It's a skill.

And like with other skills, a bit of focused, informed effort offers a reliable, if unsexy, path toward improvement.

Notes

1. **Note how "almost" helps writers reach toward a more extreme word without fully committing to it.**

    "Oswaldo was flummoxed by the fact that his friend could be so quiet, <u>almost</u> embarrassed, about his academic acumen, yet so damn loud and proud of his status as a premier campus drug dealer."

    —Jeff Hobbs, *The Short and Tragic Life of Robert Peace* (2014)

    "Next to it was Bergman Bags and Hats, which must have remained unchanged in terms of its interior and range from the day it was founded in the forties, and Radio City, which had just gone bankrupt, but you could still see a window full of illuminated TV screens, surrounded by a wide selection of electrical goods, with prices written on large, <u>almost</u> luminous orange-and-green bits of cardboard."

    —Karl Ove Knausgaard, *My Struggle (Book 2): A Man in Love* (2013)

2. **Note how "even" functions in a similar way.**

    "Their more extreme admirers will tell you that imagination and invention are outmoded contrivances; that to inhabit the subjectivity of a character unlike the author is an act of appropriation, <u>even</u> colonialism; that the only authentic and politically defensible mode of narrative is an autobiography."

    —Jonathan Franzen, introduction to *The Best American Essays* (2016)

"There, he began to feel some actual joy, <u>even</u> exhilaration, which made him want to leap forward and grab every woman who vaguely resembled the latest pictures she had sent him, all of which he had neatly framed and hung on the walls of his room."
—Edwidge Danticat, "Seven" (2001)

3. Note how "almost" is sometimes set off by dashes.
"Our dawning Age of Anxiety is perfectly symbolized by the mysterious—the <u>almost</u> mystical—figure of Benjamin Nathan Cardozo."
—Grant Gilmore, *The Ages of American Law* (1977)

4. Note how "even" is sometimes set off by dashes.
"Both my father and my grandmother believed that Jagu's and Rejsh's mental illnesses had been precipitated—<u>even</u> caused, perhaps—by the apocalypse of Partition, its political trauma sublimated into their psychic trauma."
—Siddhartha Mukherjee, *The Gene: An Intimate History* (2016)

5. Notice how "almost" often comes after one adjective to form a pair.
"He looked startled, <u>almost</u> afraid."
—Octavia Butler, *Fledgling* (2005)

6. Note how "even" often comes after one adjective to form a pair.
"They were thick, <u>even</u> plump looking hands, and they moved in the same inarticulate, blind way if they picked up a salt shaker or the handle of a suitcase."
—Patricia Highsmith, *The Price of Salt, or Carol* (1952)

7. **Note how "almost" occasionally comes after two adjectives to form a series.**
"One could scarcely read these lines in any other than a quiet, musing, <u>almost</u> whispered way."
—Mary Oliver, *A Poetry Handbook* (1994)

8. **Note how "even" occasionally does too.**
"The choices we discern as having been made in the Constitutional Convention impose burdens on governmental processes that often seem clumsy, inefficient, <u>even</u> unworkable, but those hard choices were consciously made by men who had lived under a form of government that permitted arbitrary governmental acts to go unchecked."
—Chief Justice Warren Burger, *INS v. Chadha* (1983)

9. **Note how "almost" doesn't have to come after any adjective. It can simply appear alone.**
"Mr. Carton's manner was so careless as to be <u>almost</u> insolent. He stood half turned from the prisoner, lounging with his elbow against the bar."
—Charles Dickens, *A Tale of Two Cities* (1859)

"The entire project, in other words, was rooted in Danny's doubts about his own work, and his willingness, which was <u>almost</u> an eagerness, to find error in that work."
—Michael Lewis, *The Undoing Project: A Friendship That Changed Our Minds* (2016)

10. **Note how "almost" and "even" can come after the words they modify, appearing in a slightly different position than in all the previous examples. Play around with both arrangements. Take advantage of each word's flexibility.**

"Reluctantly, Jay got out of the car. Instead of heading for the club, though, he just stood there, staring at Tim, pleading <u>almost</u>, as if he wanted to be talked out of what he was about to do. But it was his choice, and Tim couldn't make it for him."
—Tom Perrotta, *The Abstinence Teacher* (2007)

"I still resent it when anyone at my table seasons something as soon as it is put before him. I know that his tongue is jaded, calloused <u>even</u>, by restaurant sauces and a thousand dinners that have had to be heightened with anything at hand in order to be swallowed at all."
—M. F. K. Fisher, "M. F. K. Fisher on the Basics" (1949)

11. **Note how "almost" and "even" can be nice additions to poems.**

"I'm greeted, mingling, and the air when it's still
momentarily turns into an earthy, <u>almost</u> stifling
cloud of mixed perfumes, of bouquets and sweat."
—Dan Howell, "Chicago Epithalamion" (2004)

"Admit you'd like to find something
discarded or damaged, <u>even</u> gone,
and lift it back into the world."
—Stephen Dunn, "Dismantling the House" (2016)

"ALMOST" AND "EVEN"

Nuance Practice*

(1) Robert Caro's multivolume chronicle of President Lyndon Johnson has been called "the highest expression of biography as art," "*the* great book about American politics in the twentieth century," and "one of America's most amazing literary achievements."  In the third volume, *Master of the Senate*, Caro uses *even* at the end of a sentence to show that although Johnson could certainly be brash and bullying, he could also exhibit other, softer qualities—at least in certain circumstances.

> In these conversations he never threatened—he had nothing to threaten with, of course—or demanded. He was respectful, deferential—_____, <u>even</u>.

Guess the missing word.

(A) hilarious
(B) humble
(C) hubristic
(D) hospitable

(2) The book *Hellhound on His Trail* by Hampton Sides examines the assassination of Martin Luther King Jr. and the international hunt for the man who committed it, James Earl Ray. In one of the opening chapters, Sides uses *almost* to describe the surprisingly tranquil setting of the Missouri

---
* For answers, see page 201 of the Answer Key.

prison from which Ray escaped in 1967, one year before using a Remington rifle to kill King with a single shot.

> More than two thousand inmates were crammed inside "Jeff City," this vast Gothic bastille, which, upon its founding in 1836, was the first U.S. prison west of the Mississippi. Over the decades, it had developed a reputation as a school for rogues—and as one of America's most violent prisons. In 1954, a team of corrections experts described riot-prone Jeff City this way: "Square foot for square foot, it is the bloodiest forty-seven acres in America." Yet the prison complex was set in a lazy, almost _____ part of the Midwest. Beyond the limestone walls, tugboats churned through the Missouri River, and Vs of geese honked in the haze along the flyway toward summer haunts.

Guess the missing word.

(A) chaotic
(B) frantic
(C) acrylic
(D) bucolic

"ALMOST" AND "EVEN"

(3) One of the more monumental works of history was written by Edward Gibbon in the eighteenth century. Spanning six volumes, it chronicles the decline and fall of a famous empire founded about seventeen hundred years earlier. Here is an excerpt from volume 3.

> But the son of Theodosius passed the slumber of his life, a captive in his palace, a stranger in his country, and the patient, <u>almost</u> the indifferent, spectator of the ruin of the Western empire, which was repeatedly attacked, and finally subverted, by the arms of the Barbarians.

Name the empire. (<u>Hint</u>: It is the same empire referenced in the sayings "_____ wasn't built in a day" and "When in ____. . . .")

(4) The following passage comes from a short story first published in 1899.

> She received Nekhludoff as if he were one of them, and her fine, <u>almost</u> imperceptible flattery made him once again aware of his virtues and gave him a feeling of satisfaction.

The author's other works include *Anna Karenina*, *The Death of Ivan Ilyich*, and *War and Peace*. Name him.

First Name: L _ _
Last Name: T _ l _ _ _ y

THREE
Chiasmus ("A-B-B-A")

"I figured out something, Lorie," he said. "I figured out why you and me get along so well. You <u>know more</u> than you <u>say</u> and I <u>say more</u> than I <u>know</u>. That means we're a perfect match, as long as we don't hang around one another more than an hour at a stretch."

—Larry McMurtry, *Lonesome Dove* (1985)

Hell was a place of remembering, each beautiful moment passed through the mind's eye until it fell to the ground like a rotten mango, <u>perfectly useless</u>, <u>uselessly perfect</u>.

—Yaa Gyasi, *Homegoing* (2016)

Overview

A favorite nuance move among my students is something called *chiasmus*. Represented by the pattern A-B-B-A, it's when a certain grammatical structure is repeated—but in a reverse order. Here's an example from the book *Born to Run* by Christopher McDougall, which chronicles a tribe of amazing long-distance runners who live near the Copper Canyon mountains in Northern Mexico.

> You don't <u>stop running</u> because you <u>get old</u>. You <u>get old</u> because you <u>stop running</u>.

Notice the A-B-B-A pattern. You'll see it again in the next example, from an ad campaign launched in 2017 by the motorcycle brand Harley-Davidson.

> <u>All</u> for <u>freedom, freedom</u> for <u>all</u>.

Readers of the French novel *The Three Musketeers* by Alexandre Dumas might see a resemblance between the Harley-Davidson phrase and the motto of Dumas's trio of protagonists.

> <u>All</u> for <u>one</u> and <u>one</u> for <u>all</u>.

But I want to clarify something, especially for those of you who may have heard of not just the term *chiasmus* but another term as well: *antimetabole*.

As Ward Farnsworth explains in that great compendium I mentioned in the introduction, *Classical English Rhetoric*, "A chiasmus need not repeat the same words in reversed order. It can instead consist just of a structural reversal, with the two halves of the device using different words that do parallel work." He offers a clever line from *Measure by Measure* by William Shakespeare as an example.

> Some <u>rise</u> by <u>sin</u>, and some by <u>virtue fall</u>.

See the reversal there? In the initial part of the sentence, we have "rise by sin." The verb (*rise*) comes before the noun (*sin*). But in the next part of the sentence, Shakespeare switches the order. Now the verb (*fall*) comes after the noun (*virtue*).

Farnsworth notes that some commentators only use the term *chiasmus* for this kind of reconfiguration, where you get the inversion of the syntax but not the repetition of the actual words. These commentators then use the more specialized term *antimetabole* for when you get both the inversion and the repetition, like the "All for one, one for all" example from the *Three Musketeers*. As for how to navigate this difference, I like Farnsworth's suggestion: "In keeping with this book's preference for simple terminology and distaste for distinctions that aren't worth the bother for the typical user, we will call all these reversals by the same name—*chiasmus*; but the reader with a taste for jargon, a need for precision, or a fear of pedants is duly notified that more words are available."

Whatever you call the move, my main hope is that you start to both notice it and use it. Just as "You don't stop running because you get old, you get old because you stop running," perhaps "You don't stop using chiasmus because you get old, you get old because you stop using chiasmus."

Notes

1. **Note how chiasmus can be used to create pithy observations.**
"<u>Grief</u> is <u>depression</u> in proportion to circumstance; <u>depression</u> is <u>grief</u> out of proportion to circumstance."
—Andrew Solomon, *The Noonday Demon: An Atlas of Depression* (2001)

"We are not <u>final</u> because we are <u>infallible</u>, but we are <u>infallible</u> only because we are <u>final</u>."
—Justice Robert Jackson, *Brown v. Allen* (1953)

2. **Note how chiasmus can be used to communicate a powerful reversal or transformation.**
"In times of peace, <u>sons</u> bury <u>fathers</u>; in times of war, <u>fathers</u> bury <u>sons</u>."
—Herodotus, *The Histories* (440 BCE)

"The circumstances leading to the change in Mr. Covey's course toward me form an epoch in my humble history. You have seen how <u>a man</u> was made <u>a slave</u>; you shall see how <u>a slave</u> was made <u>a man</u>."
—Frederick Douglass, *Narrative of the Life of Frederick Douglass, an American Slave* (1845)

3. **Note how chiasmus can be used to highlight a dilemma.**
"If both the law and the constitution apply to a particular case, so that the court must either decide that case conformably to <u>the law</u>, disregarding <u>the constitution</u>; or conformably to <u>the constitution</u>, disregarding <u>the law</u>: the court must determine which of these conflicting rules governs the case."
—Justice John Marshall, *Marbury v. Madison* (1803)

CHIASMUS ("A-B-B-A")

"In Paris we have a <u>beautiful existence</u> but not a <u>full life</u>, and in New York we have a <u>full life</u> but an <u>unbeautiful existence</u>."
—Adam Gopnik, *Paris to the Moon* (2000)

4. **Note how chiasmus can be used to make distinctions.**
"Paul De Man may have been a <u>scoundrel</u> who found a career teaching a certain <u>method of reading</u>, but that <u>method of reading</u> does not turn people into <u>scoundrels</u>."
—Louis Menand, "The De Man Case" (2014)

"We had <u>too much greed</u> and <u>too little fear</u>. Now we have <u>too much fear</u> and <u>too little greed</u>."
—Lawrence Summers, quoted by Nate Silver in *The Signal and the Noise* (2012)

5. **Note how chiasmus can lead to new ideas, or at least new framing of ideas.**
"Instead of doing <u>a check-in</u> that had <u>an optional photo</u>, we thought, Why don't we do <u>a photo</u> that has <u>an optional check-in</u>?"
—Instagram CEO Kevin Systrom, quoted by Kara Swisher in "The Money Shot" (2013)

"We don't <u>hire people</u> to <u>make brownies</u>. We <u>make brownies</u> to <u>hire people</u>."
—Greyston Bakery, company website (2017)

"Ask not what <u>your country</u> can do for <u>you</u>; ask what <u>you</u> can do for <u>your country</u>."
—John F. Kennedy, inaugural address (1961)

6. **Note how chiasmus is kid-friendly.**

    "I <u>meant</u> what I <u>said</u> and <u>said</u> what I <u>meant</u>. An elephant's faithful one-hundred percent."
    >—Dr. Seuss, *Horton Hatches the Egg* (1940)

    "For the strength of the <u>pack</u> is the <u>wolf</u>. The strength of the <u>wolf</u> is the <u>pack</u>."
    >—Rudyard Kipling, "The Law for the Wolves" (1895)

    "The <u>wonderful thing</u> about <u>tiggers</u> is that <u>tiggers</u> are <u>wonderful things</u>."
    —A. A. Milne, "Winnie the Pooh and the Blustery Day" (1968)

CHIASMUS ("A-B-B-A")

Nuance Practice*

(1) Match the slogan with the company that created it.

Slogan	Company
"Love the Taste. Taste the Love."	John Deere
"The King of Hotels and the Hotel of Kings"	Southwest Airlines
"It's Not How Fast You Mow; It's How You Mow Fast."	Ritz-Carlton
"No Change Fees: Because Sometimes 9–5 becomes 5–9"	Jimmy John's

(2) Credit for establishing the scientific method often goes to a British philosopher who, in his 1605 book *The Advancement of Learning*, wrote that "if a man will begin with <u>certainties</u>, he shall end in <u>doubts</u>; but if he will be content to begin with <u>doubts</u>, he shall end in <u>certainties</u>."

Fill in his name: Sir Francis _____.

(A) Pythagoras
(B) Copernicus
(C) Einstein
(D) Bacon

---

* For answers, see page 202 of the Answer Key.

(3) The following passage from the 1935 novel *It Can't Happen Here* was written by the first American to win the Nobel Prize in Literature.

> "Yes!" said Emil Staubmeyer. "Didn't Hitler save Germany from the Red Plague of Marxism? I got cousins there. I *know*!"
>
> "Hm," said Doremus, as often Doremus did say it. "Cure the evils of Democracy by the evils of Fascism! Funny therapeutics. I've heard of their <u>curing syphilis</u> by giving the <u>patient malaria</u>, but I've never heard of their <u>curing malaria</u> by giving the <u>patient syphilis</u>!"

(A) Toni Morrison
(B) Rabindranath Tagore
(C) Sinclair Lewis
(D) J. K. Rowling

(4) Peter Drucker was one of the most revered management thinkers of the twentieth century. His ability to make pithy, memorable distinctions can be seen in the following excerpt from his 1963 book *Managing for Business Effectiveness*.

> It is fundamentally the confusion between effectiveness and efficiency that stands between doing the <u>right</u> <u>things</u> and doing _____ _____. There is surely nothing quite so useless as doing with great efficiency what should not be done at all.

Complete the missing chiasmus.

FOUR

"If"—"If"—"If Not"

If our minds are those of hunter-gatherers, our cuisine is that of ancient farmers.
—Yuval Noah Harari, *Sapiens: A Brief History of Humankind* (2011)

There was no money in my budget to afford restaurant food, so my son and I were often loyal, if unhappy, diners at Chez Jefferson.
—Maya Angelou, *Hallelujah! The Welcome Table: A Lifetime of Memories with Recipes* (2004)

But what if the typical hospital nurse or bank teller gets curious and starts questioning how things are done? Outside of some truly exceptional places like Google and IBM and Corning, curiosity is unwelcome, if not insubordinate.
—Charles Fishman and Brian Grazer, *A Curious Mind: The Secret to a Bigger Life* (2015)

Overview

The move in this chapter is actually three moves. Each involves the word *if*. Sometimes the *if* comes at the beginning of a sentence, like in *Seven Brief Lessons on Physics* by the Italian theoretical physicist Carlo Rovelli.

> <u>If</u> [Max] Planck is the father of the theory, [Albert] Einstein is the parent who nurtured it.

Other times the *if* comes in the middle of a sentence. The book *Autobiography of a Face* by the Irish American poet Lucy Grealy has a good example.

> They treated me respectfully, <u>if</u> somewhat distantly, though there was a clique of boys who always called me names.

There are even situations in which the *if* will be paired with the word *not*. An essay on bitcoin in the *London Review of Books* by the English writer John Lanchester contains one of those.

> Just as the Civil War was the prompt for the United States to end private money, and the crisis of Kenyan democracy led to the explosive growth of M-Pesa, the global financial crisis seems to have been a crucial spur, <u>if not</u> to the development of bitcoin, then certainly to the timing of its launch.

The Notes section will help further distinguish these various uses of *if*. It will also illustrate that one of them—*if not*—shares a lot in common with the two moves we encountered in chapter 2: *almost* and *even*. I mention this overlap because the more you start to see connections (and differences) between the growing set of moves we're learning, the better you'll become at figuring out when and how to use each one.

Notes

1. **Note how "if" at the beginning of a sentence can establish a stylish comparison.**

   "If F.D.R. was their hero, Marcus Garvey was their God."
   —Paule Marshall, "From the Poets in the Kitchen" (1983)

   "If Edwin Arlington Robinson brought American poetry into the twentieth century, it was his fellow New Englander Robert Frost who would make the decisive break from the inflated style of Victorian and genteel poetry."
   —Christopher Beach, *The Cambridge Introduction to American Poetry* (2003)

2. **Note how this kind of "if" is sometimes preceded by the word "but."**

   "But if [David] Ben-Gurion's remark about 'the connection between the Nazis and some Arab rulers' was pointless, his failure to mention present-day West Germany in this context was surprising."
   —Hannah Arendt, *Eichmann in Jerusalem: A Report on the Banality of Evil* (1963)

   "But if thought corrupts language, language can also corrupt thought."
   —George Orwell, "Politics and the English Language" (1946)

3. **Note how a different kind of "if" can be used in the middle of a sentence, as a way to talk back to and refine the word (or words) that come before it.**

   "The blue jeans fashion truly exploded in the 1950s, propelled to new heights by the hit 1955 movie *Rebel Without a Cause* and its handsome star James Dean, who died at age twenty-four, a

month before the movie was released, while driving his sports car recklessly. The death was perfect, _if_ ghoulish, publicity for the movie."
>—Robert Shiller, *Narrative Economics: How Stories Go Viral and Drive Major Economic Events* (2019)

"To Elizabeth, Lord James sent an obsequious _if_ highly perceptive letter, regretting Mary had ever 'taken in head to pretend interest or claim title' to the English throne."
—John Guy, *Queen of Scots: The True Life of Mary Stuart* (2004)

4. **Note how using "if not" instead of "if" has a way of stretching the description toward a more extreme characterization.**
"From Baghdad, Mosul is viewed with suspicion _if not_ outright hostility."
>—Ghaith Abdul-Ahad, "The Baghdad Road" (2017)

"It is necessary for a bull fighter to give the appearance, _if not_ of prosperity, at least of respectability, since decorum and dignity rank above courage as the virtues most highly prized in Spain, and bull fighters stayed at the Luarca until their last pesetas were gone."
>—Ernest Hemingway, "The Capital of the World" (1936)

"IF"—"IF"—"IF NOT"

Nuance Practice*

(1) In *The Wizard of Lies*, former *New York Times* journalist Diana Henriques examines the man behind the elaborate Ponzi scheme that cost investors more than 50 billion dollars in the early 2000s. She uses *if* at the beginning of a sentence to emphasize just how different the perception of Wall Street was when this man was growing up, back in the 1950s.

> <u>If</u> investing on Wall Street seemed unwise, working there looked like a remote possibility at best for kids like _____ _____ in the 1950s—and not just because it was risky. Nobody made much money as a stock broker in the late 1940s and early 1950s, when government bonds were far more attractive to shell-shocked investors than corporate stocks.

Identify the man.

(A) Gordon Gecko
(B) Bernie Madoff
(C) Jay Gatsby
(D) Charles Foster Kane

---

* For answers, see page 202 of the Answer Key.

(2) The focus of *Janesville: An American Story* by Pulitzer Prize winner Amy Goldstein is the manufacturing town of Janesville, Wisconsin. Goldstein uses *if* to highlight the role two large companies played in the town's development. Fill in the missing phrase.

> <u>If</u> Parker Pen put Janesville on ____ ____, GM kept it there. It proved that Janesville could surmount adversity under trying circumstances, seemingly immune to the blows of history.

(A) the hot seat
(B) the payroll
(C) the map
(D) the bandwagon

Nuance Review: "If Not" vs. "Almost" vs. "Even"

Students often make the following mistake when trying to learn a subject or skill: they move on to new material too quickly, without taking time to reflect on and consolidate old material. So this book is periodically filled with "Nuance Review" sections where you'll get a chance to connect and compare the most recent nuance move (*if not*) with ones covered in earlier chapters—in this case, *almost* and *even* from chapter 2.

You'll notice that each of the moves is very similar. Don't worry if you have a tough time distinguishing them. What's more important is that you start to recognize when at least one of them might help you better communicate your ideas.

(1) The first example comes from the novel *Human Acts* by Han Kang, a South Korean writer who won the Man International Book Prize in 2016.

> Your hair is cropped short. You are wearing jeans and ultramarine sneakers. The sleeves of your pale gray shirt are just long enough to cover your elbows, and at the top of your back the sweat-soaked fabric has darkened to an inky black. In spite of your androgynous outfit, your small frame and slender neck make you seem delicate, _____ fragile.

(A) if not
(B) almost
(C) even

(2) The second example comes from a nonfiction book about dolphins by Susan Casey, the former editor-in-chief of Oprah Winfrey's magazine O. A review in *USA Today* described the book, which is called *Voices in the Ocean*, as "painstakingly researched and gorgeously written." A review in the *Guardian* came to a similar conclusion: "What starts out as a feel-good, new-agey account darkens like the sunlight diminishing in the deep, subtly turning into a devastating chronicle of one of the most egregious mismatches in natural-human history. The result is a brilliantly written and passionate book." Complete the following sentence from the book itself.

> After decades of out-of-the-box "participatory research" with dolphins, and quite against the odds, she had forged a prosperous, ___ settled, existence.

(A) if not
(B) almost
(C) even

FIVE

"As"

The computer crash was <u>as</u> total <u>as</u> it was mysterious. The waiting lines grew restive.
—Salman Rushdie, *The Golden House* (2017)

A greater obstacle, <u>as</u> impassable <u>as</u> it was unforeseen, obliged a new and indefinite postponement.
—Gabriel García Márquez, *One Hundred Years of Solitude* (1967)

Overview

The nuance move we are going to learn in this chapter involves using the word *as* to make a balanced comparison. Here's an example from *God Help the Child* by Toni Morrison, who became, in 1993, the first African American woman to win the Nobel Prize in Literature.

> A taxi was preferable because parking a Jaguar in that neighborhood was <u>as</u> dim-witted <u>as</u> it was risky.

See how the degree to which that parking decision was "dim-witted" is made to match the degree to which it was "risky"? The *as* gives Morrison a chance to make those two judgments at once.

You can see something similar in the next example. It comes from *Behold the Dreamers* by Imbolo Mbue, who grew up in Limbe, Cameroon, and now lives in New York City.

> Winston hired a lawyer for him, a fast-talking Nigerian in Flatbush, Brooklyn, named Bubakar, who was <u>as</u> short <u>as</u> his speech was fast.

Later in that same book, Mbue uses the *as* move again. This time she doubles up the comparison.

> He hung up and sighed, a sigh <u>as</u> deep and audible <u>as</u> it was hopeless and defeated.

You'll see more examples of that and other variations in the Notes section. My hope is that they will each be as helpful as they are interesting.

"AS"

Notes

1. **Note how "as" can be used to create a balanced comparison between people, particularly if those people have opposite characteristics.**

"Jessner eventually started to dig into hundreds of violent crimes linked to the Aryan Brotherhood. Working with an officer from the Bureau of Alcohol, Tobacco and Firearms named Mike Halualani—a half-Japanese, half-Hawaiian agent who was <u>as</u> brash <u>as</u> Jessner was genteel—Jessner attempted to devise a strategy to break the gang's stranglehold."
—David Grann, *The Devil and Sherlock Holmes* (2010)

"The Sandinistas in Nicaragua appear to be <u>as</u> skillful in consolidating power <u>as</u> the Ayatollah Khomeini is inept, and leaders of both revolutions display an intolerance and arrogance that do not bode well for the peaceful sharing of power or the establishment of constitutional governments, especially since those leaders have made clear that they have no intention of seeking either."
—Jeane Kirkpatrick, "Dictatorships and Double Standards" (1979)

2. **Note how "as" can also be used to create a balanced comparison between qualities in the same person.**

"The unhappy Hook was <u>as</u> impotent <u>as</u> he was damp, and he fell forward like a cut flower."
—J. M. Barrie, *Peter Pan* (1904)

"Thou art <u>as</u> wise <u>as</u> thou art beautiful."
—William Shakespeare, *A Midsummer Night's Dream* (1605)

3. **Note how "as" can be used to provide a double compliment—or a double insult.**

"The decision by both the Constitution's Framers and the 1886 Congress to minimize this Court's role in resolving close federal Presidential elections is <u>as</u> wise <u>as</u> it is clear."
—Justice Stephen Breyer, dissenting, *Bush v. Gore* (2000)

"<u>As</u> vain <u>as</u> he was treacherous, White was heard to boast, 'I am the Nicaragua Transit company!'"
—T. J. Stiles, *The First Tycoon: The Epic Life of Cornelius Vanderbilt* (2009)

4. **Note how "as" can be used to compare more than just a couple of qualities.**

"With a heart full of love and gratitude, I now take leave of you. I most devoutly wish that your latter days may be <u>as</u> prosperous and happy <u>as</u> your former ones have been glorious and honorable."
—General George Washington, "Farewell Address to His Army at Fraunces Tavern" (1783)

"It was for this reason that the late glorious queen, who on all accounts was formed to produce general love and admiration, and whose life was <u>as</u> mild and beneficent <u>as</u> her death was beyond example great and heroic, became so very soon and so very much the object of an implacable rancor, never to be extinguished but in her blood."
—Edmund Burke, *Letters on a Regicide Peace* (1796)

"AS"

Nuance Practice*

(1) One of the landmark cases in the history of gay rights is an 1895 trial involving charges of homosexuality against a famous Irish writer. While being cross-examined, the writer gave an eloquent explanation of a line in ones of his poems that reads "I am the Love that dare not speak its name."

> The "Love that dare not speak its name" in this century is such a great affection of an elder for a younger man as there was between David and Jonathan, such as Plato made the very basis of his philosophy, and such as you find in the sonnets of Michelangelo and Shakespeare. It is that deep, spiritual affection that is <u>as</u> pure <u>as</u> it is perfect. It dictates and pervades great works of art like those of Shakespeare and Michelangelo, and those two letters of mine, such as they are.

Unscramble the following letters to find out the name of the writer.

First Name: CSAOR
Last Name: DIWLE

---

* For answers, see page 203 of the Answer Key.

(2) Jelani Cobb is a staff writer for the *New Yorker* and a professor of journalism at Columbia University. In the passage below, he discusses a famous novel by Ralph Ellison that is taught on campuses throughout the country and commemorated with a statue on 150th Street and Riverside Drive in Harlem, near where Ellison lived for much of his life.

> In _____, published in 1952, Ralph Ellison, who was a student at Tuskegee Institute in the nineteen-thirties, described the tense dynamic between black colleges and their leadership. The first section of the novel is set at an unnamed Southern school, where the protagonist, a student, runs afoul of the president, Dr. Bledsoe, who is <u>as</u> dictatorial toward blacks <u>as</u> he is deferential to whites.

Identify the novel.

(A) *Native Son*
(B) *Sula*
(C) *Their Eyes Were Watching God*
(D) *Invisible Man*

"AS"

Nuance Practice: Henry Kissinger*

Surely no statesman in modern times, and certainly no American secretary of state, has been as revered and then as reviled as Henry Kissinger.
—Niall Ferguson,
Kissinger: 1923–1968: The Idealist (2015)

(1) **Isaacson on Kissinger:** "No matter what Kissinger would say in the future, no matter how strong his arguments might appear, [South Vietnam President Nguyen Van] Thieu would never again trust him. The rationales Kissinger later gave for misleading Thieu were as numerous as they were _____."
—Walter Isaacson, *Kissinger: A Biography* (2005)

(A) unobtrusive
(B) unattractive
(C) unconvincing
(D) unintelligible

(2) **Dallek on Kissinger:** "Their optimism was as _____ as it was boundless."
—Robert Dallek, *Nixon and Kissinger: Partners in Power* (2007)

(A) unwise
(B) unconscious
(C) unassuming
(D) unheralded

---

* For answers, see page 203 of the Answer Key.

(3) **Kissinger on Kissinger:** "What made the Syrian-Israeli shuttle as moving as it was _____ was that in the process each side caught at least a glimpse of the truth that the only hope of their future lay in coexistence."

—Henry Kissinger, *Years of Upheaval* (1982)

    (A) topical
    (B) timid
    (C) torrential
    (D) tortuous

SIX
Nuance Spotlight

JANE AUSTEN
(1775–1817)

Jane Austen is one of the great writers of English literature because no reader and no period exhausts her books. Something always escapes from a reading while every reading enriches. Like the town of Lyme in Persuasion, *the novels "must be visited, and visited again."*

—Janet Todd, *The Cambridge Introduction to Jane Austen* (2006)

Overview

Now that we have learned a number of individual moves in the previous five chapters, we are going to change things up a bit and put a kind of spotlight on a writer who deftly uses a whole bunch of them. We'll periodically do these Nuance Spotlights as we move through the book. They can be a nice way to both review the material and appreciate the skill and range of various authors.

We'll start with the eighteenth-century British novelist Jane Austen, who is so beloved by her fans that some use bumper stickers to express their admiration, a common one being "I'd rather be reading Jane Austen." Other devotees rush to the movie theater any time one of her books gets adapted into a film. And a few have even taken on the task of creating modern retellings of her now famous plots and characters, as the best-selling author Curtis Sittenfeld did in *Eligible*, a novel that sets *Pride and Prejudice* in suburban Cincinnati and adds the backdrop of a reality TV show.

There is good reason for all this adulation. In addition to being an astute observer of social manners and aspirations, Austen is a supremely gifted crafter of sentences. The modernist poet Ezra Pound once told a writer that he should use Austen as his benchmark for what to keep in his own draft. "Read [the draft]," Pound said, "and kick out every sentence that isn't as Jane Austen would have written it." Along these same lines, the British writer Margaret Drabble suggests that "there would be more genuine rejoicing at the discovery of a complete new novel by Jane Austen than any other literary discovery, short of a new major play by Shakespeare."

The Notes section contains examples from Austen's most famous works—*Emma*, *Pride and Prejudice*, and *Sense and Sensibility*—as well as from a few lesser known ones. When it comes to nuance, Austen had an endless supply.

Notes

1. Un-

"The extreme sweetness of her temper must hurt his. He had all the clearness and quickness of mind which she wanted, and he could sometimes act <u>ungracious</u>, or say a severe thing."

—Jane Austen, *Emma* (1815)

"My dear Sir Thomas, with all my faults I have a warm heart; and, poor as I am, would rather deny myself the necessaries of life than do an <u>ungenerous</u> thing."

—Jane Austen, *Mansfield Park* (1814)

"In one point, her feelings were relieved by this knowledge of Mr. Elliot. There was no longer anything of tenderness due to him. He stood as opposed to Captain Wentworth, in all his own unwelcome obtrusiveness; and the evil of his attentions last night, the irremediable mischief he might have done, was considered with sensations <u>unqualified</u>, <u>unperplexed</u>."

—Jane Austen, *Persuasion* (1817)

2. Almost

"There is an openness, a quickness, <u>almost</u> a bluntness in Mr. Weston, which everybody likes in *him*, because there is so much good humour with it—but that would not do to be copied."

—Jane Austen, *Emma* (1815)

3. If not

"This argument was irresistible. It gave to his intentions whatever of decision was wanting before; and he finally resolved, that it would be absolutely unnecessary, <u>if not</u> highly indecorous, to do more for the widow and children of his father, than such kind of neighbourly acts as his own wife pointed out."

—Jane Austen, *Sense and Sensibility* (1811)

"They made their appearance in the Lower Rooms; and here fortune was more favourable to our heroine. The master of the ceremonies introduced to her a very gentlemanlike young man as a partner; his name was Tilney. He seemed to be about four or five and twenty, was rather tall, had a pleasing countenance, a very intelligent and lively eye and, <u>if not</u> quite handsome, was very near it."

—Jane Austen, *Northanger Abbey* (1817)

4. As

"Wholly inattentive to her sister's feelings, Lydia flew about the house in restless ecstasy, calling for everyone's congratulations, and laughing and talking with more violence than ever; whilst the luckless Kitty continued in the parlour repined at her fate in terms <u>as</u> unreasonable <u>as</u> her accent was peevish."

—Jane Austen, *Pride and Prejudice* (1813)

"If my sister, in the security of retirement, with <u>as</u> little opportunity <u>as</u> inclination to do evil, could not avoid censure, we must not rashly condemn those who, living in the world and surrounded with temptations, should be accused of errors which they are known to have the power of committing."

—Jane Austen, *Lady Susan* (1871)

SEVEN

"At Once"

The sight of big ships, of the men in their uniforms, <u>at once</u> serious and cool, left [George] Bush with an overall sense of the navy's power and camaraderie and purpose as he returned north to school.

—Jon Meacham, *Destiny and Power: The American Odyssey of George Herbert Walker Bush* (2015)

It's <u>at once</u> humbling and stirring to imagine just how expansive reality may be.

—Brian Greene, *The Hidden Reality: Parallel Universes and the Deep Laws of the Cosmos* (2011)

Overview

The phrase *at once* can create a nice rhythmic balance. Consider the following example from the memoir *Things I've Been Silent About*. It's by Iranian author Azar Nafisi, who also wrote the popular book *Reading* Lolita *in Tehran*.

> It took me some time to accept the fact that my father's family had its own secrets and untruths. They were <u>at once</u> intellectually adventurous and extremely puritanical.

See how "intellectually adventurous" and "extremely puritanical" have the same structure?

- Adverb ("intellectually") adjective ("adventurous")
- Adverb ("extremely") adjective ("puritanical")

That's not an accident. Nor is it an accident when the literary critic Ruth Franklin uses the same grammatical arrangement in a 2018 article about the Norwegian writer Karl Ove Knausgaard and his monumental six-volume opus *My Struggle*.

> Its 3,600-some pages, <u>at once</u> weirdly self-deprecating and breathtakingly egoistic, began to appear in English, at the rate of a volume a year, in 2012, culminating this fall with the translation of Book Six.

- Adverb ("weirdly") adjective ("self-deprecating")
- Adverb ("breathtakingly") adjective ("egoistic")

Additional varieties appear in the Notes section. Test out a bunch to find out which ones work best for you. You'll soon discover that the move can be at once playful and elegant.

Notes

1. **Note how "at once" can be used to communicate how a person or group has two somewhat oppositional characteristics.**
   "She was <u>at once</u> a heroine—although she disdained that word, too—and a flawed and average person."
   —Tilar Mazzeo, *Irena's Children: The Extraordinary Story of the Woman Who Saved 2,500 Children from the Warsaw Ghetto* (2016)

   "Al Qaida's approach was <u>at once</u> too patient and too hasty."
   —Graeme Wood, *The Way of the Strangers: Encounters with the Islamic State* (2016)

2. **Note how "at once" is sometimes paired with alliteration.**
   "The hazy and murmuring countryside, the moon, the decline of the evening, stirred within me. Going down the gently sloping road I could not feel fatigue. The evening was <u>at once</u> intimate and infinite."
   —Jorge Luis Borges, "The Garden of Forking Paths," translated by Anthony Kerrigan (1941)

   "Some of the most memorable moments as a chef—<u>at once</u> revelatory and revealing—are provoked by tasting something delicious."
   —Dan Barber, *The Third Plate: Field Notes on the Future of Food* (2014)

3. **Note how "at once" can be used to create a double whammy.**
   "Like the schoolyard bully, our criminal justice system harasses people on small pretexts but is exposed as a coward before murder. It hauls masses of black men through its machinery

but fails to protect them from bodily injury and death. It is <u>at once</u> oppressive and inadequate."
   —Jill Leovy, *Ghettoside: A True Story of Murder in America* (2015)

"His function was a responsible one, <u>at once</u> onerous and thankless, and his fidelity in it the greater because of his strong patriotic impulse."
   —Herman Melville, *Billy Budd* (1924)

4. **Note how "at once" can be combined with the Rule of Three.***
   "Naturally, Felix [Rohatyn]'s desperate effort to escape, which began in Vienna in 1935 and ended in New York City in 1942, seared into him an inviolate worldview. He is <u>at once</u> preternaturally pessimistic about the outcome of events, extremely conservative financially, and far less prone to excessive ostentation than most of his extremely wealthy investment banking peers."
   —William Cohan, *The Last Tycoons: The Secret History of Lazard Frères & Co.* (2007)

5. **Note how "at once" can be combined with the much less often used Rule of Four (or More).**
   "Then she showed him her hands, flung them out in a gesture <u>at once</u> spontaneous and diffident and self-conscious and proud, and told him he might bring her an orange stick."
   —William Faulkner, *Sanctuary* (1931)

---

* If you want to learn more about the Rule of Three, check out chapter 3 of *Good with Words: Writing and Editing*. I cover it in more detail there. You can access a free electronic version of the book at the following URL: https://www.fulcrum.org/concern/monographs/1v53jz538.

"And it's the tone here that kills, <u>at once</u> searching and mocking and vulnerable, amused and amusing."
—Justin Torres, "The Way We Read Now" (2018)

6. **Note how an alternative to "at once" is "simultaneously."**
"But when I glanced at the people around us, no one was even looking in our direction, and I felt the way I often felt in this country—<u>simultaneously</u> conspicuous and invisible, like an oddity whom everyone noticed but chose to ignore."
—Cristina Henríquez, *The Book of Unknown Americans* (2014)

"He's almost giddy, yammering as he often does but in a brighter mood and with greater control than usual, bubbling with images that are <u>simultaneously</u> daffy and brilliant."
—Steve Lopez, *The Soloist: A Lost Dream, an Unlikely Friendship, and the Redemptive Power of Music* (2008)

Nuance Practice*

(1) The focus of Dava Sobel's 2016 book *The Glass Universe* is a group of women at the Harvard Observatory who transformed the field of astronomy. Fill in the blank with the word that Sobel pairs with *supplement* in the *at once* sentence below.

> Within the Bruce telescope's first few months of operation in Peru, it produced photographic charts of the entire southern sky. These images <u>at once</u> supplemented and _____ the existing southern star catalogues.

(A) implemented
(B) augmented
(C) tormented
(D) fermented

(2) Nathalia Holt's *Rise of the Rocket Girls* also centers around women and space. Her specific interest is the set of expert female mathematicians who were hired by NASA to help launch the first American satellites and generally speed up exploration of the solar system in the years following World War II. Unscramble the letters below to see how Holt uses *at once* to highlight the dual qualities of a gyroscope, which is a tool used to stabilize astronomical readings in equipment like the Hubble Telescope.

> The gyroscope seemed to defy gravity, <u>at once</u> spinning around an axis and stubbornly _____ direction.

Scrambled: NGMATINAINI
Unscrambled: _____

---

* For answers, see page 203 of the Answer Key.

"AT ONCE"

(3) In 1952, during the middle of the Korean War, a massive railroad strike in Youngstown, Ohio, led to a constitutional showdown in which the Supreme Court placed important limits on presidential power. Here is an excerpt from the majority opinion.

> They acted on the conviction that the experience of man sheds a good deal of light on his nature. It sheds a good deal of light not merely on the need for effective power if a society is to be <u>at once</u> cohesive and civilized, but also on the need for limitations on the power of governors over the governed.

The US president at the time, whose attempt to seize control of the railroad triggered the case, remained angry at the Court's decision for years. Yet he put that anger aside, at least temporarily, when one of the justices, Hugo Black from Alabama, invited him to dinner soon after the decision was filed. "Hugo," the president supposedly said at one point, "I don't care much for your law, but by golly, this bourbon is good." Name this president.

First Name: _ A _ _ Y
Last Name: T _ _ M _ _

(4) The following two uses of *simultaneously*—a word we said can substitute for *at once*—are taken from Khaled Hosseini's best-selling novel about Afghanistan.

- "General Taheri managed a simultaneously sad and polite smile, heaved a sigh, and gently patted Baba's shoulder."
- "'I thought you were getting Cokes,' Baba said, taking the bag of peaches from me. He was looking at me in a simultaneously serious and playful way. I began to make something up, but he bit into a peach and waved his hand. 'Don't bother, Amir. Just remember what I said.'"

Name the novel: *The Kite* _____.

(Hint: The novel was turned into a popular movie with the same title in 2007.)

EIGHT

"Equal Parts"

When Ebony *launched the 100 Most Influential Black Americans in April 1971, my dad, John H. Johnson, wanted to highlight and celebrate the most outstanding African Americans for their contributions across multiple disciplines. Today, I say with <u>equal parts</u> love, pride, and respect, that my dad was exactly the kind of individual the list was established to recognize.*
—Linda Johnson Rice, "CEO's Letter: The Class of 2017" (2017)

Another marcher was her old classmate from Englewood High, artist Margaret Taylor, a self-described "young radical," petite, unstoppable, and constantly creative, <u>equal parts</u> Nina Simone and Frida Kahlo, with enough brass and sass for both of them.
—Thomas Dyja, The Third Coast: When Chicago Built the American Dream (2013)

Overview

In the previous chapter, we learned how the phrases *at once* and *simultaneously* can be used to bring together unlike elements. In this chapter, we'll add another term to that category: *equal parts*. The first example comes from Lisa Ko's novel *The Leavers*, which was a finalist for the National Book Award in Fiction in 2017.

> I saw how much Didi would miss me if I left. I would miss her, too, though I already missed her, the way we had been when we only had each other, believing that being the oldest residents at the boardinghouse was a thing to be proud of, when the ambiguity of our lives was terrifying and enthralling, when each new day was <u>equal parts</u> fear and opportunity.

The second example comes from another highly acclaimed book: *The Black Count: Glory, Revolution, and the Real Count of Monte Cristo* by Tom Reiss. It won the Pulitzer Prize in Biography in 2013.

> Claude Labouret, who had begun referring to his son-in-law as "the General," must have been <u>equal parts</u> astonished, proud, and intimidated by the rapid transformation of young Alex from mounted cavalryman to commander-in-chief.

Notice in the example from *The Black Count* that *equal parts* brings together not just two elements but three: *astonished*, *proud*, and *intimidated*. This variation shows that *equal parts*, like many of the moves we've learned, has some versatility. Take advantage of its range.

"EQUAL PARTS"

Notes

1. **Note how "equal parts" can be used to capture a mix of emotions.**
   "As I forced her to try on dress after dress hand-selected by the stylish hands of Mimi Melgaard, Betsy kept giving me the eye, equal parts amused and horrified at the dreamlike joy on my face."
   —Shonda Rhimes, *Year of Yes* (2016)

   "He's drunk and crushed as he calls her name. In the end she stops, turns with her fists clenched, and stares at him, her tears now caused by equal parts exposure and fury."
   —Fredrik Backman, *Beartown* (2016)

2. **Note how "equal parts" is often followed by two terms.**
   "'Only now do I see how madly in love with you I am!' The relationship, as expressed in their letters, remained equal parts intellectual and emotional, but the emotional part was now filled with a fire unexpected from a self-proclaimed loner."
   —Walter Isaacson, *Einstein: His Life and Universe* (2007)

   "He bade his neighbors good-bye. 'I leave here tomorrow for Washington, and shall probably see but few of you again for some years to come.' He added, with equal parts tact and sincerity: 'It would give me great pleasure to make an annual pilgrimage to a place where I have enjoyed myself so much as I have here during the past few months.'"
   —H. W. Brands, *The Man Who Saved the Union: Ulysses Grant in War and Peace* (2012)

3. **Note how "equal parts" can also be followed by three terms.**
   "[Woodrow Wilson] proceeded to deliver a stirring inaugural address. Equal parts lesson, sermon, and mission statement,

his carefully chosen 1,800 words—composed over the last month—began with a simple proclamation of fact: 'There has been a change of government.'"
—A. Scott Berg, *Wilson* (2013)

4. **Note how "equal parts" will occasionally come at the end of a sentence.**
"Kubrick needed somebody who had knowledge and imagination in equal parts."
—Dan Chiasson, "*2001: A Space Odyssey*: What It Means, and How It Was Made" (2018)

5. **Note how the *Washington Post* likes to use "equal parts" in its headlines.**
"With 'Detroit,' Kathryn Bigelow Refines an Aesthetic Grounded in Equal Parts Theory and Reality"
—*Washington Post*, July 27, 2017

"Equal Parts Blisters and Enlightenment"
—*Washington Post*, August 9, 2006

"Equal Parts Idiocy and Idealism"
—*Washington Post*, July 8, 1989

6. **Note how "equal measures" can achieve the same effect as "equal parts."**
"Meeting settlers for the first time in these bourgeois utopias, I felt like I was the token minority at an upscale New York City party; I could feel myself being scrutinized with equal measures of fascination and curiosity, and not a small quotient of horror. The settlers were friendly, a bit guarded and standoffish at first, but mostly curious why a guy who looked like a Long Island Uber driver had come to Israel to talk with them."
—Wajahat Ali, "A Muslim Among Israeli Settlers" (2018)

"EQUAL PARTS"

Nuance Practice*

(1) In *Katrina: After the Flood*, Pulitzer Prize–winning journalist Gary Rivlin chronicles the recovery effort that followed the hurricane that devastated New Orleans in 2005. He uses an *equal parts* formulation to describe one of the residents he interviewed, Mitch Landrieu.

> Mitch Landrieu turned forty-five two weeks before Katrina. He was trim with short-cropped gray hair and piercing blue eyes. His thick, butterscotch New Orleans accent seemed <u>equal parts</u> _____ and movie tough guy.

Pick the missing phrase.

(A) old North
(B) old South
(C) new North
(D) new South

(2) In her 2014 memoir *The Art of Asking*, the musician Amanda Palmer frequently shares stories about Anthony Martignetti, a writer and psychotherapist committed to supporting the local arts scene in Boston, where Palmer got her start. At one point, Palmer uses *equal parts* to express the bundle of emotions their time together produced, after Martignetti became extremely sick.

> My visits with Anthony had grown more intense since his illness and scare at the hospital, and I started looking forward to them with <u>equal parts</u> joy and _____.

---

* For answers, see page 203 of the Answer Key.

I wasn't just hanging out with my best friend; I was hanging out with a sick person.

Which word goes in the blank?

- (A) drama
- (B) worry
- (C) jingoism
- (D) relief

Nuance Review: "Equal Parts" vs. "At Once"

We now know that the phrases *equal parts*, *at once*, and *simultaneously* do similar work. The next set of sentences shows that it is not always easy to determine which option the author chose.

(1) "I've always been lucky enough to be suffered by people much wiser than I. When I was in eighth grade, I had an English teacher, _____ kind and intelligent, who was ever-ready to entertain my tragically uninformed views of President Obama."
—Christian Alejandro Gonzalez, "Academia Needs Conservative Professors" (2018)

    (A) equal parts
    (B) at once
    (C) simultaneously

(2) "A gun wielded by a marching white supremacist leads a complicated double life, for it is _____ deadly and expressive."
—David M. Shapiro, "Guns, Speech, Charlottesville: The Semiotics of Semiautomatics" (2017)

    (A) equal parts
    (B) at once
    (C) simultaneously

(3) "As a result, *Just Mercy* [by Bryan Stevenson] is a remarkable amalgam, _____ a searing indictment of American criminal justice and a stirring testament to the salvation that fighting for the vulnerable sometimes yields."
—David Cole, "The Disgrace of Our Criminal Justice" (2014)

    (A) equal parts
    (B) at once
    (C) simultaneously

NINE

"To"

New technologies and growing urbanization have made it easier than ever to bring people together in both real and virtual spaces to share ideas, make new things, and join forces on projects of all kinds. At the same time, emerging forms of unbundling, from jobs <u>to</u> cars <u>to</u> homes <u>to</u> entertainment, have refined the slices in which we produce and consume.

—Lee Fennell, *Slices and Lumps: Division and Aggregation in Law and Life* (2019)

From building shelters <u>to</u> shooting ink <u>to</u> changing color, the vulnerable octopus must be ready to outwit dozens of species of animals, some of which it pursues, others it must escape.

—Sy Montgomery, *The Soul of an Octopus: A Surprising Exploration into the Wonder of Consciousness* (2015)

Overview

The preposition *to* can helpfully link three items, as in the following sentence about Thomas Jefferson from the book *American Creation* by historian Joseph Ellis.

> To be sure, Jefferson was a sincere aficionado of all things Gallic, from French cooking <u>to</u> Parisian architecture <u>to</u> revolutionary politics.

But although three items seems to be this move's sweet spot, it can also link both less than three items and more than three items. Here's an example where *to* links less than three items. It comes from the book *Biased* by Stanford sociologist Jennifer Eberhardt.

> Bias can lead to racial disparities in everything from preschool suspensions <u>to</u> corporate leadership.

As for linking more than three items, James Forman Jr., a former public defender who now teaches at Yale Law School, does that in *Locking Up Our Own*, a book that won the Pulitzer Prize for General Nonfiction in 2018.

> From felon disenfranchisement laws that suppress black votes, <u>to</u> exploitative housing practices that strip black wealth, <u>to</u> schools that refuse to educate black children, <u>to</u> win-at-all-costs prosecutors who strike blacks from jury pools, <u>to</u> craven politicians who earn votes by preying on racial anxieties, <u>to</u> the unconscious and implicit biases that infect us all, it is impossible to understand American crime policy without appreciating racism's enduring role.

A similarly extreme example appears in *The Triumph of Christianity: How a Forbidden Religion Swept the World* by Bart Ehrman, a historian of religion who teaches at the University of North Carolina. The author of a number of best-selling books, Ehrman uses the *to* move to explain the pervasive role gods played during the fourth century, when the emperor Constantine made his influential conversion to the Christian faith.

> On the practical level, the gods were understood to be closely connected with every aspect of the social and political life of a community, from the election of officials, to the setting of the annual calendar, to the law and practices that governed social relations, such as marriage and divorce, to the administration of civil justice, to the decisions and actions of war, to all the other major decisions of state.

You don't need to match the length of Ehrman's list to use *to* effectively. There is no Guinness World Record for "Most Instances of *To* in a Sentence." (And even if there were, I doubt the winning entry would be the kind of writing we'd want to emulate.) But as you'll discover in the Notes section, there is a wide range of ways the move can be deployed. So search around. Try a few that seem promising. And then perhaps see if you can come up with your own. The categories in this and other sections of the book are merely starting points. Expand on and improve any you think are worth changing.

Notes

1. **Note how "to" can cover and connect a large range of material.**

   "The conception of political equality from the Declaration of Independence, to Lincoln's Gettysburg Address, to the Fifteenth, Seventeenth, and Nineteenth Amendments can mean only one thing—one person, one vote."
   —Justice William O. Douglas, *Gray v. Sanders* (1963)

   "Throughout this vast republic, from the St. Croix to the Gulf of Mexico, from the Atlantic to the Pacific, revenue is to be collected and expended, armies are to be marched and supported."
   —Chief Justice John Marshall, *McCulloch v. Maryland* (1819)

2. **Note how "to" works well with a list of three items.**

   "This technique can be used in nearly any area: put together a group of people all interested in the same thing—or join an existing group—and use the group's camaraderie and shared goals as extra motivation in reaching your own goals. This is the idea behind many social organizations, from book clubs to chess clubs to community theaters, and joining—or, if necessary, forming—such a group can be a tremendous way for adults to maintain motivation."
   —Anders Ericsson and Robert Pool, *Peak: Secrets from the New Science of Expertise* (2016)

3. **Note how "to" can also work well with just two items.**

   "For now, [Martin Luther King Jr.'s] notion of leadership emphasized the display of learning. He said many wise things in his address—on technology, colonialism, the pace of time,

but the speech as a whole went sprawling. King quoted notables from Heraclitus to Bob Hope."
—Taylor Branch, *Parting the Waters: America in the King Years 1954–1963* (1988)

4. **Note how "to" is often combined with alliteration.**
"Venture capitalists have poured money into start-ups aiming to disrupt everything from lingerie to luggage to lipstick, with less emphasis on the product than on the scope of the ambition and the promise of tech-enabled efficiencies."
—Bianca Bosker, "Mayonnaise, Disrupted" (2017)

"From Boston to Bordeaux, revolution was in large measure the achievement of networks of wordsmiths."
—Niall Ferguson, *The Square and the Tower: Networks and Power, from the Freemasons to Facebook* (2017)

5. **Note how "to" sometimes appears with commas and sometimes doesn't. The difference seems to be how fast you want the reader to get through the list.**
"This meant he was involved in everything from designing user interfaces, to testing with customers and reviewing specifications, to coordinating with engineers."
—Jake Knapp and John Zeratsky, *Make Time* (2018)

"As always, we illustrate these translations using a wide range of applications, everything from fixing leaky toilets to increasing charitable giving to finding a job or mate."
—Barry Nalebuff and Ian Ayres, *Why Not? How to Use Everyday Ingenuity to Solve Problems Big and Small* (2003)

6. **Note how "to" can be helpful when crafting online bios and similar descriptions of experience and expertise.**
   "From Seoul to Krakow to Vancouver, Professor Cohen has spoken at legal, medical, and industry conferences around the world and his work has appeared in or been covered on PBS, NPR, ABC, CNN, MSNBC, *Mother Jones*, the *New York Times*, the *New Republic*, the *Boston Globe*, and several other media venues."

   —faculty bio for Professor I. Glenn Cohen, Harvard Law School (2019)

   "Mr. Horwich has briefed and argued cases before all levels of the federal courts, including arguing 10 cases in the Supreme Court of the United States. His industry experience ranges from pharmaceuticals, medical devices, and food production and marketing, to banking, surface and air transportation, semiconductors, and energy."

   —attorney bio for Benjamin J. Horwich, Munger, Tolles & Olson (2019)

7. **Note how "to" can also connect more than two or three items.**
   "The implications of writing signals into the brain, or 'neuromodulation,' however, were far more wide-reaching than that: being able to control neural firing would conceivably allow treatment of a host of currently untreatable or intractable neurological and psychiatric diseases, from major depression to Huntington's to schizophrenia to Tourette's to OCD . . . the possibilities were limitless."

   —Paul Kalanithi, *When Breath Becomes Air* (2016)

"TO"

Nuance Practice*

(1) Match the passage to its source.

Passage

- "Today Apache is one of the most successful open-source tools, powering about two-thirds of the web sites in the world. And because Apache can be downloaded for free anywhere in the world, people from Russia to South Africa to Vietnam use it to create web sites."
- "Several generations of start-ups have tapped these dynamics to build dominant positions, from eBay to Facebook to Airbnb. To accomplish these goals, it's critical to develop a rigorous understanding of how network effects work."
- "But when, in late March, they finally made it to the Oval Office to lay out what they thought financial reform should look like—from executive compensation practices, to the dissolution of systematically dangerous companies, to the fast-growing industry, derivatives trading—Obama was noncommittal, saying he couldn't speak with that 'level of specificity' about reform. He'd left the problem of blocked nominees untended."

Source

- Thomas Friedman, *The World Is Flat* (2005)
- Ron Suskind, *Confidence Men: Wall Street, Washington, and the Education of a President* (2011)
- Chris Yeh and Reid Hoffman, *Blitzscaling: The Lightning-Fast Path to Building Massively Valuable Companies* (2018)

---

* For answers, see page 204 of the Answer Key.

(2) In *Women and Power: A Manifesto*, Oxford historian Mary Beard includes a section on the Me Too movement. Here are a couple of sentences from it.

> I certainly hope that people will one day look back to the autumn of 2017 as the moment that kick-started a social and sexual revolution. From the casting couch to the gropes behind the office photocopier, from New York to _____, the spirit of Me Too may ensure that women are no longer silent about this kind of abuse.

Fill in the blank.

(A) New England
(B) Nairobi
(C) Cambridge
(D) New Jersey

TEN

"Albeit"

According to my father, he wanted me to learn the meaning of hard work up close and personal so that I would know what life was really like, but also because he wanted me to experience what he had gone through growing up on the outskirts of town with six siblings, odd jobs, and no help from the government. In short, I was living a version of his life, <u>albeit</u> in reverse.

—Saïd Sayrafiezadeh, "Audition" (2018)

Overview

The word *albeit* can be tricky to say. The first time one of my friends encountered it she pronounced it as *al-bate*. She used two syllables, not the standard three: *al-be-it*.

But don't let trouble with the word's phonetics stop you from trying to use it, particularly if you want to qualify a claim or description. Like the *if* move we learned in chapter 4 and the *however* move we will be learning about in chapter 11, *albeit* allows you to talk back to and refine previous information in your sentence.

A good example comes from the polymath Daniel Tammet, whose language skills, computation abilities, and staggering feats of memory were the subject of the 2005 documentary *Extraordinary People: The Boy with the Incredible Brain*. The example appears in Tammet's book *Every Word Is a Bird We Teach to Sing*, which is a collection of engaging essays on human communication.

> For the first time in my life I spoke aloud in my numerical language (<u>albeit</u>, necessarily, in English words), at length, passionately, fluently.

Tammet inserts the *albeit* between parentheses. But you can also combine it with other forms of punctuation. The coauthors of a leading textbook on constitutional law, for example, combine it with a comma in the following sentence about a series of appointments to the Supreme Court.

> Those appointments led to a more conservative Court and brought some significant changes of direction, <u>albeit</u> of disputed scope.

Matthew Cobb, a professor of zoology at the University of Manchester, makes a similar choice in a 2017 article in the *New York Review of Books* on gene editing.

But the ability to use genetic testing when deciding whether or not to have children is clearly a form of soft eugenics, <u>albeit</u> one carried out voluntarily by those affected and clearly leading to a reduction of human suffering.

You'll see other variations in the Notes section, including examples that incorporate dashes. Test out each of these options. Find the best fit for whatever you want your sentence to accomplish. "Albeit" isn't the fanciest of moves, but it can be quite helpful.

Notes

1. **Note how "albeit" can help communicate an important qualification or caveat.**
   "Degenhart would survive, <u>albeit</u> with a nearly pulverized left elbow."
   —Sebastian Rotella, "A Gunfight in Guatemala" (2016)

   "With her tidy shoulder-length hair and polo shirt, Emily Harris looks like the open-faced midwestern college student she recently was, <u>albeit</u> one with an ammunition belt slung across her chest."
   —Jeffrey Toobin, *American Heiress: The Wild Saga of the Kidnapping, Crimes, and Trial of Patty Hearst* (2016)

2. **Note how "albeit" often comes at the end of a sentence, after the main point has been made.**
   "The excitement she felt was all the greater because she was excited against her will. In other words, her soul did condone the proceedings, <u>albeit</u> covertly."
   —Milan Kundera, *The Unbearable Lightness of Being* (1984)

   "Bishop's business started to turn around, <u>albeit</u> slowly."
   —Morten Hansen, *Great at Work: How Top Performers Do Less, Work Better, and Achieve More* (2018)

3. **Note how "albeit" can also start a sentence.**
   "And since her new routine of saving was pretty easy, they decided they'd start making a dent in other bills they had, like student loans. <u>Albeit</u> change wasn't felt overnight, they started to make headway and progress was made just the same."
   —Tony Hsieh, *Delivering Happiness* (2010)

4. **Note how "albeit" is frequently surrounded by commas.**
"In the criminal justice system, there are various constraints, albeit imperfect, to filter out insubstantial legal claims."
—Justice Anthony Kennedy, *Cheney v. United States District Court for the District of Columbia* (2004)

"But Joe had the gun barrel up now, albeit shakily, and tried to maneuver his horse around to angle for a shot."
—James McBride, *Song Yet Sung* (2008)

5. **Note how "albeit" can also be surrounded by dashes or even parentheses.**
"She was an anonymous housewife—albeit an extraordinary one—flattered by the attention of a famous writer."
—Ruth Franklin, *Shirley Jackson: A Rather Haunted Life* (2016)

"We never went to church, except on rare occasions in Kentucky or when Mom decided that what we needed in our lives was religion. Nevertheless, Mamaw's was a deeply personal (albeit quirky) faith. She couldn't say 'organized religion' without contempt."
—J. D. Vance, *Hillbilly Elegy* (2016)

Nuance Practice*

(1) In *Endure: Mind, Body, and the Curiously Elastic Limits of Human Performance*, Cambridge-trained physicist Alex Hutchinson examines how top athletes "struggle to continue against the mounting desire to stop." Sometimes this struggle leads to amazing feats: completing ultramarathons, climbing Mt. Everest, breaking world records. But other times it leads to disaster, as Hutchinson describes in the following passage.

> According to a tally kept by the National Center for Catastrophic Sport Injury Research, a total of 143 football players died from heatstroke between 1960 and 2016. The vast majority of those deaths were high schoolers, and they generally took place during summer practice, when the weather was hottest and the players were least fit. But even pros are not immune: the heatstroke death of Minnesota Vikings offensive tackle Korey Stringer, during a training camp in 2001, put the issue on front pages around the country, <u>albeit</u> _____.

Pick the missing word.

(A) deftly
(B) permanently
(C) briefly
(D) intermittently

---

* For answers, see page 205 of the Answer Key.

(2) In *The Smartest Kids in the World,* journalist Amanda Ripley travels to schools in Finland, Poland, and South Korea to explore how various educational systems compare with ones in the United States. The passage that follows focuses on how teachers are selected and trained.

> Interestingly, Korean elementary teachers were not always so carefully chosen. For many years, the teachers in training attended less prestigious two-year colleges. But, in the early 1980s, those education colleges became four-year universities offering more rigorous training and boosting the status of the profession. This history is almost identical to the story of Finland, which also consolidated its middling training programs into the more elite university system (albeit a _____ or so earlier). . . . This proven approach—elevating the selectivity and rigor of the teaching profession at the very beginning of teachers' careers—has never been attempted on a large scale in the United States, despite its obvious logic.

Pick the missing word.

(A) month
(B) year
(C) decade
(D) century

(3) Match the use of *albeit* with its source.

Examples

- "Today, there are some 115 index mutual funds designed to track the S&P 500 Index. Astonishingly, more than half of them carry an initial sales load, albeit often concealed by offering class 'B' shares with no front-end load but with an additional heavy annual fee (used to pay the broker)."
- "While we can never know what would have happened if the Court had not acted as it did (if *Brown* had never been decided or had come out the other way), the existence and strength of the pro-civil-rights forces at least suggest that change would have occurred, albeit at a pace unknown."
- "We must not accept the state of corruption as if it were just another sin. Even though corruption is often identified with sin, in fact they are two distinct realities, albeit interconnected."

Source

- John Bogle, *The Little Book of Common Sense Investing* (2007)
- Gerald N. Rosenberg, *The Hollow Hope: Can Courts Bring About Social Change?* (1991)
- Pope Francis, *The Name of God Is Mercy* (2016)

ELEVEN

"However"

He liked being connected with them, <u>however</u> tenuously.

—Zadie Smith, *White Teeth* (2000)

<u>However</u> wide awake they may have been before they entered that sleepy region, they are sure, in a little time, to inhale the witching influence of the air, and begin to grow imaginative, to dream dreams, and see apparitions.

—Washington Irving, "The Legend of Sleepy Hollow" (1820)

Overview

Often when we use the word *however*, it's to single out some sort of contrast, like in the sentence below from *Silent Spring* by Rachel Carson, who is frequently credited with helping start the modern environmental movement.

> These natural cancer-causing agents are still a factor in producing malignancy; however, they are few in number and they belong to that ancient array of forces to which life has been accustomed from the beginning.

But I want to introduce a different, more nuanced use of *however*. You can think of it as the equivalent of saying something like "no matter how." Here's an example from *Capitalism and Freedom* by the Nobel Prize–winning economist Milton Friedman.

> However attractive anarchy may be as a philosophy, it is not feasible in a world of imperfect men.

No matter how attractive anarchy may be as a philosophy, Friedman is saying, it is not feasible in a world of imperfect men. You can try and try and try, he suggests, but it's just not going to work.

Notice that Friedman uses this version of *however* at the beginning of a sentence. The move can also appear in the middle of a sentence or at the end of one, as the next two examples illustrate. Both reveal something else as well: it is not uncommon for skilled writers to double up their use of *however*. We'll start with when the *howevers* come in the middle of a sentence, using an excerpt from *The Map That Changed the World* by the British journalist Simon Winchester.

> The ideas of Steno and Hooke, however hostile their initial reception by the Church, however flaccid their initial acceptance by the public, began slowly to take root.

To now see what it is like to put *howevers* at the end of a sentence, we can turn to an article written in the *Texas Monthly* by John Phillip

Santos, a longtime resident of San Antonio and the first Mexican American to win a Rhodes Scholarship. He is describing an intellectual feud between two chroniclers of Texas history: Américo Paredes and J. Frank Dobie.

> In short, even by the time Paredes wrote his lacerating critique, Dobie seemed to be evolving, however slowly, however imperfectly.

Two final examples are worth mentioning. The first, from the theologian Reinhold Niebuhr, shows that you can even split your *howevers* if you'd like: one at the middle, one at the end. The result is a nice bit of parallel structure.

> But unfortunately ultimate perils, however great, have a less lively influence upon the human imagination than immediate resentments and friction, however small by comparison.

The second example, from historian Gordon Wood and his book *Friends Divided: John Adams and Thomas Jefferson*, is a fun reminder that doubling your *howevers* might not be enough. Sometimes you'll want to triple them.

> However true, however correct, however in accord with stubborn facts Adams's ideas might have been, they were incapable of inspiring and sustaining the United States, or any nation for that matter.

But even if you just stick to a single *however*, take a chance on working one into your sentences. There is a lot more to the word than its standard role as a pivot point and sign of contrast.

Notes

1. **Note how "however" can be used to communicate something like the phrase "no matter how."**
"To get Firefox or Chrome, you have to demonstrate some resourcefulness and download a different browser. Instead of accepting the default, you take a bit of initiative to seek out an option that might be better. And that act of initiative, <u>however</u> tiny, is a window into what you do at work."
—Adam Grant, *Originals: How Non-Conformists Move the World* (2016)

"Though the crocuses poke up their heads in the usual places,
The frog scum appear on the pond with the same froth of green,
And boys moon at girls with last year's fatuous faces,
I never am bored, <u>however</u> familiar the scene."
—Theodore Roethke, "Vernal Sentiment" (1904)

2. **Note how skilled writers create a nice rhythm by using "however" twice in a row.**
"Because in the end to learn a language, to feel connected to it, you have to have a dialogue, <u>however</u> childlike, <u>however</u> imperfect."
—Jhumpa Lahiri, *In Other Words* (2015)

"Pathetic as it felt, Jacob was jealous. Julia's cruel comments—<u>however</u> accurate, <u>however</u> deserved—lingered painfully in his mind."
—Jonathan Safran Foer, *Here I Am* (2016)

"But I knew that <u>however</u> bitter my regret, and <u>however</u> well the pineal operation went, nothing I could do would undo the damage that I had done to the young woman."
—Henry Marsh, *Do No Harm: Stories of Life, Death, and Brain Surgery* (2014)

3. **Note how this "no matter how" use of "however" can come at the beginning of a sentence.**

"<u>However</u> long we postpone it, we eventually lie down alone in that notoriously uncomfortable bed, the one we make ourselves."
—Joan Didion, *Slouching Towards Bethlehem* (1968)

4. **Note how "however" has a rich history in Supreme Court opinions.**

"But if an act is within the powers specifically conferred upon Congress, it seems to me that it is not made any less constitutional because of the indirect effects that it may have, <u>however</u> obvious it may be that it will have those effects, and that we are not at liberty upon such grounds to hold it void."
—Justice Oliver Wendell Holmes Jr., *Hammer v. Dagenhart* (1918)

"Working conditions are obviously local conditions. The employees are not engaged in or about commerce, but exclusively in producing a commodity. And the controversies and evils which it is the object of the act to regulate and minimize are local controversies and evils affecting local work undertaken to accomplish that local result. Such effect as they may have upon commerce, <u>however</u> extensive it may be, is secondary and indirect. An increase in the greatness of the effect adds to its importance. It does not alter its character."
—Justice George Sutherland, *Carter v. Carter Coal Co.* (1936)

"Section 922(q) is a criminal statute that by its terms has nothing to do with 'commerce' or any sort of economic enterprise, <u>however</u> broadly one might define those terms."
—Chief Justice William Rehnquist, *United States v. Lopez* (1995)

"If a friend asked you 'to get her tart lemons, sour lemons, or sour fruit from Mexico,' you might well think her list of terms perplexing: You might puzzle over the difference between tart and sour lemons, and wonder why she had specifically mentioned lemons when she apparently would be happy with sour fruit of any kind. But of one thing, you would have no doubt: Your friend wants some produce *from Mexico*; it would not do to get her, say, sour lemons from Vietnam. <u>However</u> weird the way she listed fruits—or the way §2252(b)(2) lists offenses—the modifying clause still refers to them all."
—Justice Elena Kagan, *Lockhart v. United States* (2016)

"HOWEVER"

Nuance Practice: Confessions*

(1) "<u>However</u> ____ a new agency may be, it must have the self-restraint to turn down moribund accounts. A surgeon with an established practice can afford to have an occasional patient die on the operating table, but a young surgeon's whole career can be ruined by such a misadventure. I used to dread having one of our accounts die on our operating table."
—David Ogilvy, *Confessions of an Advertising Man* (1963)

(A) hungry
(B) ignorant
(C) just
(D) correct

(2) "For after it was clear that he was ignorant of those arts in which I thought he excelled, I began to despair of his opening and solving the difficulties which perplexed me (of which indeed, <u>however</u> _____, he might have held the truths of piety, had he not been a Manichee)."
—St. Augustine, *The Confessions of St. Augustine*, translated by E. B. Busey (397–400 CE)

(A) hungry
(B) ignorant
(C) just
(D) incorrect

---

* For answers, see page 206 of the Answer Key.

(3) "Or suppose, even more simply, that Samuel Turner—<u>however</u> decent and _____ an owner he might have remained anyway—had been less affected with that feverish and idealistic conviction that slaves were capable of intellectual enlightenment and enrichment of the spirit and had not, in his passion to prove this to himself and to all who would bear witness, fastened upon *me* as an 'experiment.'"
　　　　　　—William Styron, *The Confessions of Nat Turner* (1967)

  (A) hungry
  (B) ignorant
  (C) just
  (D) incorrect

"HOWEVER"

Nuance Practice: World War II*

(1) The following sentence is taken from a dissent in one of the most notorious Supreme Court cases in history. It was written in the middle of World War II, when over 120,000 Japanese Americans were forced to live in internment camps.

> To give constitutional sanction to that inference in this case, <u>however</u> well-intentioned may have been the military command on the Pacific Coast, is to adopt one of the cruelest of the rationales used by our enemies to destroy the dignity of the individual and to encourage and open the door to discriminatory actions against other minority groups in the passions of tomorrow.

The author of the dissent is Justice Robert Jackson. The case is _____.

  (A) *Dred Scott v. Sandford*
  (B) *Plessy v. Ferguson*
  (C) *Korematsu v. United States*
  (D) *Bradwell v. Illinois*

(2) In 2012, British journalist Max Hastings was awarded a prize from the Pritzker Military Library for his lifetime achievement in military writing. Among his many books on World War II is *Inferno: The World at War, 1939–1945*. An excerpt is below. Fill in the blank.

> The Nazis, <u>however</u> _____, conceded a free hand in the east to the Soviets, whose objectives included

---

* For answers, see page 206 of the Answer Key.

eastern Finland and the Baltic states in addition to a large share of Poland's carcass.

(A) indelicately
(B) indefinitely
(C) impossibly
(D) insincerely

(3) In *Memoirs of the Second World War*, one of the most important figures of World War II describes the "mortal need" Allied forces faced.

> The mortal need was Security at all costs and by all methods, however stern or even harsh.

Two years after that memoir was published, the author was awarded the Nobel Prize in Literature for his "mastery of historical and biographical description as well as for his brilliant oratory in defending exalted human values."

Name him. (Hint: He is the only prime minister to win the Nobel Prize in Literature.)
First Name: W _ _ s _ _ n
Last Name: _ _ u _ c _ i _ l

TWELVE

"At Best, At Worst"

Up and to the left, you can see a dark patch where the wall meets the ceiling. It seems like the spot is <u>at best</u> damp and <u>at worst</u> crumbling.

—Kathryn J. Edin and H. Luke Shaefer, *$2.00 a Day: Living on Almost Nothing in America* (2015)

September 1797. The boy would be dead before dawn. He was fifteen, more handsome already than his famously handsome father, who had turned back toward New York City when he received the news. <u>At best</u>, the boy's father would arrive in time to hold his son's hand as the end came. <u>At worst</u>, he would arrive only in time to embrace his grieving wife.

—Victoria Johnson, *American Eden: David Hosack, Botany, and Medicine in the Garden of the Early Republic* (2018)

Overview

The paired phrases *at best* and *at worst* create a helpful evaluative range. You can think of them as establishing a ceiling for the most positive option and a floor for the most negative option. Take, for example, a sentence from Walter Isaacson's biography of Leonardo da Vinci.

> Some critics have suggested that [da Vinci's] excess of diagrams showing light hitting contoured objects and his deluge of notes about shadows were <u>at best</u> a waste of time and <u>at worst</u> led him to be too studied in some later works.

The most positive option—the *at best*—is that da Vinci's diagrams and notes were simply "a waste of time." The most negative option—the *at worst*—is that those diagrams and notes actually harmed da Vinci's artistic execution later on in his career. By using these phrases as rhetorical markers, Isaacson makes the boundaries of critical opinion clear.

You'll learn in the Notes section that you have some freedom when it comes to structuring *at best* / *at worst* constructions. You can start with *at best* and then end with *at worst*, as Isaacson did in his sentence about da Vinci. You can also start with *at worst* and then end with *at best*. You can even drop one of the phrases altogether and just go with the other.

Tara Westover picks this third option in *Educated*, her best-selling memoir about growing up in a family that subscribed to extreme apocalyptic beliefs, including not allowing her to attend school. "<u>At best</u> I was two people, a fractured mind," she writes toward the end of the book, describing her conflicted thoughts and feelings when she returns to her family's home in the mountains of Idaho. There is no corresponding *at worst*.

Perhaps the most interesting use of *at best* / *at worst* I've come across, however, is in an essay the *New York Times* columnist Wesley

Morris wrote in April 2019 about the decline in romantic comedies as a popular movie genre. Typically, writers use *at best / at worst* within the same sentence. But Morris stretches it over several sentences.

He begins with an evaluative floor in one sentence, using a version of *at worst*. He then waits until 12 sentences later to deliver the evaluative ceiling, using a version of *at best*. In between, he tosses in 21 commas, 2 parentheses, 3 dashes, 2 colons, 1 exclamation point, and 222 words.

> At its worst, these movies could be painfully formulaic, corny, retrograde about gender and so unrealistic about love that they were often accused of poisoning real-life romance. (Back in 2008, a study in Scotland concluded that watching them can create unrealistic expectations of romantic partners.) *Good riddance*, you might cry. *Enjoy your spot in antiquity! Say hi to westerns for me.*
>
> I have no serious rebuttal to any of these objections. They're mostly true. I'm a single black gay man, and therefore an unlikely champion of the American romantic comedy: What's in these movies for me?
>
> And yet here I am, in a state of panicked rumination: Who are we without these movies? Romantic comedy is the only genre committed to letting relatively ordinary people—no capes, no spaceships, no infinite sequels—figure out how to deal meaningfully with another human being. These are the lowest-stakes movies we have that are also about our highest standards for ourselves, movies predicated on the improvement of communication, the deciphering of strangers and the performance of more degrees of honesty than I ever knew existed—gentle, cruel, blunt, clarifying, T.M.I., strategic, tardy, medical, sexual, sartorial. They take our primal hunger to connect with one

another and give it a story. <u>And at their best</u>, they do much more: They make you believe in the power of communion.

None of the examples in the Notes section approach Wesley's level of separation. But all will, I hope, give you a sense of how useful—and versatile—*at best / at worst* can be.

Notes

1. **Note how the order of "at best" and "at worst" can switch. Sometimes "at best" comes first. Sometimes "at worst" comes first.**

   "This mode of representation is called primitivism. For many of these black artists, Africa was not a place or a source of formal inspiration; it was <u>at best</u> a theme, <u>at worst</u> a fad. No one indirectly or otherwise actually became African."

   —Henry Louis Gates Jr., *Stony the Road: Reconstruction, White Supremacy, and the Rise of Jim Crow* (2019)

   "Gen was so central to the way he thought now that Mr. Hosokawa forgot sometimes he didn't know the languages himself, that the voice people listened to was not his voice. He had not understood what the man with the gun was saying and yet it was perfectly clear to him. <u>At worst</u>, they were dead. <u>At best</u>, they were looking at the beginning of a long ordeal."

   —Ann Patchett, *Bel Canto* (2001)

2. **Note how although "at best" and "at worst" often come at the beginning of a key phrase, they can also come after it.**

   "Think of the transitive verbs for sex—the ones that fit in the slot *John verbed Mary*. . . . They're not very nice, are they? The verbs are jocular or disrespectful <u>at best</u> and offensive <u>at worst</u>. So what are the verbs that we do use in polite company when referring to the act of love?"

   —Steven Pinker, *The Stuff of Thought: Language as a Window into Human Nature* (2005)

"Our democracy can work only if voters know how the world works, so they are able to make intelligent policy choices and are less apt to fall prey to demagogues, ideological zealots, or conspiracy buffs who may be confusing them <u>at best</u> or deliberately misleading them <u>at worst</u>."
—Thomas L. Friedman, *Thank You for Being Late: An Optimist's Guide to Thriving in the Age of Accelerations* (2016)

3. **Note how "at best" can sometimes appear without "at worst."**
"President Engstrom agreed with counsel David Aronofsky that the university did the right thing by not reporting the February 10 rape to Missoula law enforcement officials. 'As is required by federal law,' he told Florio, 'the university cannot and did not release the names of alleged victims or perpetrators to police.' The accuracy of this statement, however, is questionable. Federal law, Montana law, and the university's policy concerning sexual assault and the privacy of victims and perpetrators are confusing <u>at best</u>, and in some regards contradictory."
—Jon Krakauer, *Missoula: Rape and the Justice System in a College Town* (2015)

"The other two ways of getting rid of bad feelings are usually less adaptive in the long run. You could delude yourself about your own behavior, choosing to believe that you are living up to your guide when you really aren't. This is basically *denial*, and it is not recommended, since it is <u>at best</u> a short-term strategy and doesn't lead to real improvement."
—Heidi Grant Halvorson and E. Tory Higgins, *Focus* (2013)

"AT BEST, AT WORST"

Nuance Practice*

(1) In 2003, the literary magazine *Granta* put the writer Hari Kunzru on its list of best young British novelists. Try to figure out the missing word in the following passage from Kunzru's 2017 novel *White Tears*. Publications as different as *GQ*, *Time*, *The Economist*, and the *San Francisco Chronicle* singled it out as one of the top books of that year.

> I was convinced that was how it would be: he'd head on into the rest of his glamorous life while <u>at best</u> I'd be chained to a photocopier in some suburban business park, <u>at worst</u> _____ in a State hospital, my ass hanging out of a backless gown.

(A) employed
(B) revered
(C) locked
(D) chained

(2) The South African psychologist Susan David developed what the *Harvard Business Review* called "a management idea of the year" in 2013: emotional agility. She then wrote a best-selling book that explores the concept in more detail. A sentence from that book is below.

> Others are acutely aware that they expend too much energy trying to contain or suppress their emotions, treating them <u>at best</u> like _____ children and <u>at worst</u> as threats to their well-being.

---

* For answers, see page 206 of the Answer Key.

Fill in the missing word.

  (A) unruly
  (B) mature
  (C) docile
  (D) well-mannered

(3) This next sentence comes from the 2014 memoir of a famous alum of *Saturday Night Live*.

> I dated a lot of really funny people. And some medium funny. The best-looking ones were medium funny <u>at best</u>—it's tough to be both.

This person also created and starred in the sitcom *Parks and Recreation*. Name her.

First Name: Amy
Last Name: _____

THIRTEEN
Nuance Spotlight

JAMES BALDWIN
(1924–87)

James Baldwin had a long and varied career in which, in addition to essays and novels, he produced plays, scripts, short stories, and children books; but he was at his artistic summit in those works that he published during the 1950s and early 1960s. Almost nothing pertaining to race relations and social turbulence escaped Baldwin's pen during this period, although he addressed a range of other subjects, including homosexuality in André Gide's novel Madeleine, William Faulkner *and desegregation, and the ideology of racial separatism espoused by the Black Muslims.*

—*Norton Anthology of African American Literature* (2004)

Overview

It's time for another one of our Nuance Spotlights, where instead of learning a new move, we review several moves using examples from a particularly skilled writer.

The initial Nuance Spotlight, in chapter 6, featured the British writer Jane Austen, whose first full novel, *Sense and Sensibility*, came out in 1811. This second Nuance Spotlight will feature the American writer James Baldwin, who began his writing career about 150 years later with the publication of *Go Tell It on the Mountain*.

One reviewer praised Baldwin's writing for possessing "crystal clearness and a passionately poetic rhythm." Another, the playwright and novelist Darryl Pinckney, focused on his sentences in particular. "There is something wild in the beauty of Baldwin's sentences and the cool of his tone, something improbable, too, this meeting of Henry James, the Bible, and Harlem." Pinckney goes on to say, "I can see the scratches in the desk in my room where I was reading 'Notes of a Native Son,' Baldwin's memoir of his hated father's death the day his father's last child was born in 1943, one day before Harlem erupted into the deadliest race riot in its history. I can feel the effects of this essay within me still."

Here's an excerpt from that memoir. It shows Baldwin using a variant of the *if* move from chapter 4, the one that involves talking back to and refining the word (or words) that come before it. Baldwin is talking about the opera *Carmen* by the French composer Georges Bizet.

> It is true that no one in the original *Carmen*, least of all Carmen and her lover, are very clearly motivated; but there it scarcely matters because the opera is able to get by on a purely theatrical excitement, a sort of papier-mâché violence, and the intense, <u>if</u> finally incredible, sexuality of its heroine.

And here's Baldwin using a different move, chiasmus, in a 1962 essay called "As Much Truth as One Can Bear." Remember that chiasmus is the move with the inverted A-B-B-A structure.

> Not everything that is <u>faced</u> can be <u>changed</u>, but nothing can be <u>changed</u> until it is <u>faced</u>.

Additional examples are included in the Notes section. If you'd like to learn more about Baldwin, I recommend the documentary *I Am Not Your Negro* by the director Raoul Peck. It was nominated for an Academy Award in 2016 and is narrated by the actor Samuel L. Jackson, who reads from Baldwin's unfinished book *Remember This House* throughout the film. That combination—Jackson's compelling voice and Baldwin's lyrical sentences—makes for some powerful cinema.

Notes

1. At Once

"For many years, I could not ask myself why human relief had to be achieved in a fashion <u>at once</u> so pagan and so desperate—in a fashion <u>at once</u> so unspeakably old and so unutterably new."

—James Baldwin, *The Fire Next Time* (1963)

2. Even

"There have been, and are, times, and places, when to speak a certain language could be dangerous, <u>even</u> fatal."

—James Baldwin, "If Black English Isn't a Language, Then Tell Me, What Is?" (1979)

3. If Not

"It is at Chez Inez that many an unknown first performs in public, going on thereafter, <u>if not</u> always to greater triumphs, at least to other night clubs, and possibly landing a contract to tour the Riviera during the spring and summer."

—James Baldwin, *Notes of a Native Son* (1955)

4. However

"It suggests that indignation and goodwill are not enough to make the world better. Clarity is needed, as well as charity, <u>however</u> difficult this may be to imagine, much less[*] sustain, toward the other side."

—James Baldwin, "The Crusade of Indignation" (1956)

5. At Best, At Worst

"There have been superficial changes, with results <u>at best</u> ambiguous and, <u>at worst</u>, disastrous."

—James Baldwin, *Notes of a Native Son* (1955)

---

[*] We'll learn about *much less* in chapter 15.

FOURTEEN

"What ___ Is To ___"

The jury vests each citizen with a kind of magistracy. It teaches everyone that they have duties toward society and a role in its government. By forcing men to be concerned with affairs other than their own, it combats individual egoism, which is to societies <u>what</u> rust <u>is to</u> metal.

—Alexis de Tocqueville, *Democracy in America* (1835)

This isn't the first time, on the internet or on Netflix, that an original production has been presented this way ... but House of Cards *is by far the best yet. It is to Netflix <u>what</u> The Sopranos <u>was to</u> HBO, <u>what</u> The Shield <u>was to</u> FX, <u>what</u> Mad Men <u>was to</u> AMC. It's an identity maker and a game changer.*

—David Bianculli, *The Platinum Age of Television* (2016)

Overview

Comparisons are tricky. But the payoff from crafting the right one can be memorably illuminating, like when the journalist Lizzie Widdicombe suggests that "data are to today's parents <u>what</u> psychoanalysis <u>was to</u> the postwar generation: a hoped-for savior." Or when the constitutional law scholar Adam Winkler writes in *We the Corporations* that "with financing from business interests, the think tanks did for corporations <u>what</u> Nader's Raiders <u>did for</u> consumers. They gathered information, analyzed it, and publicized it to the public and to lawmakers to influence legislation."

Both of these comparisons rely on the same structure: what ____ is to _____. An example from *The Second Machine Age* by Erik Brynjolfsson and Andrew McAfee, who run MIT's Initiative on the Digital Economy, highlights how the construction works.

> Computers and other digital advances are doing for mental power—the ability to use our brains to understand and shape our environments—<u>what</u> the steam engine and its descendants <u>did for</u> muscle power.

Part of the appeal of this move is the parallel structure. There is a rhythmic symmetry that makes the comparison easy to absorb and remember, as I hope becomes clear when you make your way through the Notes section.

"WHAT __ IS TO __"

Notes

1. **Note how "what ___ is to ____" can be used to make clever comparisons.**

   "Deprivation is for me <u>what</u> daffodils <u>were for</u> Wordsworth."
   —Philip Larkin, *Required Writing: Miscellaneous Pieces, 1955–1982* (1983)

   "Perusing telegraph manuals reveals that Morse code is to the semicolon <u>what</u> weedkiller <u>is to</u> the dandelion. Punctuation was charged at the same rate as words, and their high price—trans-Atlantic cables originally cost a still-shocking $5 per word—meant that short, punchy lines with minimal punctuation were necessary among businessmen and journalists."
   —Paul Collins, "Has Modern Life Killed the Semicolon?" (2008)

   "To nutritionists, [convenience stores] are to obesity <u>what</u> drug dens <u>were to</u> the crack epidemic."
   —Michael Moss, *Salt Sugar Fat: How the Food Giants Hooked Us* (2013)

2. **Note how "what ___ is to ____" can be used to provide context, especially to audiences who might not understand certain background information.**

   "Involuntary dismissal <u>does to</u> plaintiffs <u>what</u> default <u>does to</u> defendants: It forces them to pursue the lawsuit to some resolution."
   —Stephen C. Yeazell and Joanna C. Schwartz, *Civil Procedure* (2018)

"This and other cases led to the founding of the Society for the Prevention of Cruelty to Children. It <u>did for</u> children <u>what</u> its sister organization <u>did for</u> animals."
—Jill Lepore, "Baby Doe: A Political History of Tragedy" (2016)

3. **Note how "what ___ is to ___" can be used in the past tense as "what ___ did for ___" or "what ___ was to ___."**

"One of the leading private military companies is Blackwater Worldwide. Erik Prince, the company's CEO, is a former Navy SEAL with an ardent faith in the free market. He rejects the suggestion that his soldiers are 'mercenaries,' a term he considers 'slanderous.' Prince explains: 'We are trying to do for the national security apparatus <u>what</u> Federal Express <u>did for</u> the postal service.'"
—Michael J. Sandel, *Justice: What's the Right Thing to Do?* (2008)

"'The *New Yorker* was to cartooning <u>what</u> the New York Yankees <u>were to</u> baseball—the Best Team,' Bob [Mankoff] explains."
—Angela Duckworth, *Grit: The Power of Passion and Perseverance* (2016)

4. **Note how a variant of "what ___ is to ___" involves using the word "as."**

"I say to you that the VCR <u>is to</u> the American film producer and the American public <u>as</u> the Boston strangler is to the woman home alone."
—Jack Valenti, "Home Recording of Copyrighted Works: Hearings before the Subcommittee on Courts, Civil Liberties, and the Administration of Justice" (1983)

"WHAT __ IS TO __"

Nuance Practice*

(1) In the early decades of the twentieth century, the photographer Edward Curtis embarked on what the *New York Herald Tribune* called the "most ambitious enterprise in publishing since the publication of the King James Bible": he lived among native peoples in the American West and  tried to document their way of life. The twenty-five-volume collection that resulted is called *The North American Indian*. Producing it wasn't cheap.

Fortunately, Curtis secured a powerful patron: the banker J. P. Morgan. The contours of this relationship are nicely explained by Timothy Egan in *Short Nights of the Shadow Catcher: The Epic Life and Immortal Photographs of Edward Curtis*. Here's how Egan uses the past tense version of *what ___ is to ___* to describe the iconic role Morgan's office building, known as the "House of Morgan," played in the financial world at the time.

> His white marble lair at 23 Wall Street was to global capitalism <u>what</u> the _____ <u>was to</u> Roman Catholicism.

Fill in the blank.

(A) Taj Mahal
(B) Vatican
(C) Western Wall
(D) Forbidden City

---

* For answers, see page 206 of the Answer Key.

(2) J. P. Morgan stars in another *what* ____ *is to* ____ move. It appears in an essay called "The Refragmentation" by celebrated entrepreneur and Silicon Valley thinker Paul Graham. Graham, whose team at the startup accelerator Y-Combinator has helped launch Airbnb, Dropbox, and many other breakthrough companies, uses Morgan as a reference point when discussing the competitive strategy of a different twentieth-century titan of industry.

> <u>What</u> J. P. Morgan <u>was to</u> the horizontal axis, _____ was to the vertical. He wanted to do everything himself.

<u>Hint</u>: This titan famously said of the Model-T cars his Michigan factories produced that customers could have them painted any color they wanted —so long as that color was black.

    (A) Walter Chrysler
    (B) Soichiro Honda
    (C) Henry Ford
    (D) Sakichi Toyoda

"WHAT __ IS TO __"

(3) Here's the opening line of a patent application by one of America's most prolific inventors. By the time of his death in 1931, he had secured more than a thousand of them.

> I am experimenting upon an instrument which does for the eye <u>what</u> the phonograph <u>does for</u> the ear.

Most famous for developing electric power and the lightbulb, this inventor's name is _____.

   (A) Nikola Tesla
   (B) George Washington Carver
   (C) Alexander Graham Bell
   (D) Thomas Edison

FIFTEEN

"Let Alone" and "Much Less"

Apart from what he wrote in his diary, we know very little about the life of Budayri, the barber of Damascus. He was too modest a man to feature in contemporary biographical dictionaries, the "who's who" of Ottoman times. His diary is all the more remarkable for that. It was unusual for tradesmen to be literate in the eighteenth century, <u>let alone</u> to leave a written record of their thoughts.

—Eugene Rogan, *The Arabs: A History* (2009)

> *Slavery is so vile and miserable an estate of man, and so directly opposite to the generous temper and courage of our nation, that it is hardly to be conceived that an Englishman, <u>much less</u> a gentleman, should plead for it.*
>
> —John Locke, *Two Treatises of Government* (1689)

Overview

The phrases *let alone* and *much less* are relatively interchangeable. Peter Godfrey-Smith, a philosopher of science at the University of Sydney, picked *let alone* to construct the following sentence in *Other Minds: The Octopus, the Sea, and the Deep Origins of Consciousness*.

> Organisms so small have a difficult time determining the direction light is coming from, <u>let alone</u> focusing on an image.

But he could have just as easily picked *much less* instead.

> Organisms so small have a difficult time determining the direction light is coming from, <u>much less</u> focusing on an image.

Similarly, Albert Marrin, a historian at Yeshiva University, chose to go with *much less* in his book *Uprooted: The Japanese American Experience During World War II*, when he wrote that "the historian's job is to explain the behavior of human beings in the past. Yet to explain is not to explain away, <u>much less</u> excuse." But switching to *let alone* could have worked just as well.

> The historian's job is to explain the behavior of human beings in the past. Yet to explain is not to explain away, <u>let alone</u> excuse.

In each of these examples, the authors seem to want a phrase that creates some distance away from a more extreme boundary. For Godfrey-Smith, the point is essentially to say, "Look, organisms so small are nowhere near the point where they can focus on an image; they have a hard enough time determining the direction light is coming from." For Marrin, it's more like, "Let's be clear. I am not saying that historians should explain away the behavior of human beings, and I am *certainly* not saying they should excuse that behavior."

Both *let alone* and *much less* offer that kind of strategic qualification. They give you a chance to be more precise and circumspect, while at the same time offering a bit of helpful emphasis. So although it can sometimes be hard to tell the difference between them, both are worth learning how to use.

Notes

1. **Note how "let alone" and "much less" can be used to point to something that seems extremely unlikely, even unattainable.**

   "'Bye Dad,' I said. We were poor Indians. It was always a struggle to find enough money to enjoy a decent life, <u>let alone</u> pay for college."

   —Sherman Alexie, *You Don't Have to Say You Love Me: A Memoir* (2017)

   "I am the only child of Emelie Salinas and Jose Lito Vargas. Shortly after they got married, it became apparent that they had been too young to wed, <u>much less</u> have a child."

   —Jose Antonio Vargas, *Dear America: Notes of an Undocumented Citizen* (2018)

2. **Note how "let alone" and "much less" can highlight a tougher standard, step, or action.**

   "There is simply no evidence that homegrown medical marijuana users constitute, in the aggregate, a sizeable enough class to have a discernable, <u>let alone</u> substantial, impact on the national illicit drug market—or otherwise to threaten the CSA regime."

   —Justice Sandra Day O'Connor, *Gonzales v. Raich* (2005)

   "He wrote letters to his editor; they were the most difficult letters John Wolf ever had to read, <u>much less</u> answer."

   —John Irving, *The World According to Garp* (1978)

   "They did not look at Sophia, <u>much less</u> try to speak to her."

   —Alice Munro, *Too Much Happiness* (2009)

3. **Note how "let alone" and "much less" often come toward the end of a sentence.**

   "Our picture of the spontaneous quantum creation of the universe is then a bit like the formation of bubbles of steam in boiling water. Many tiny bubbles appear, and then disappear again. These represent mini-universes that expand but collapse again while still of microscopic size. They represent possible alternate universes, but they are not of much interest since they do not last long enough to develop galaxies and stars, <u>let alone</u> intelligent life."

   —Stephen Hawking and Leonard Mlodinow, *The Grand Design* (2010)

"There were plenty of clerical attacks on *The Origin of Species*, but they were so civil and rhetorically well mannered that the new agnostics didn't cringe in fear of an angry God, <u>much less</u> a vengeful one."

—Tom Wolfe, *The Kingdom of Speech* (2016)

4. **Note how they can, however, show up in the middle of a sentence.**

   "At one point, when discussing the improbability of his Gosse biography ever being finished, <u>let alone</u> published, he paused and dropped his voice."

   —Julian Barnes, *Flaubert's Parrot* (1984)

"Soldiers on those bases might go an entire tour without ever leaving the wire, <u>much less</u> firing a gun, and grunts look down on them almost as much as they look down on the press corps."

—Sebastian Junger, *War* (2010)

"Then [*New York Times* food critic Craig Claiborne] came to our house for dinner, and I served a recipe from one of his cookbooks, a Chilean seafood-and-bread casserole that was a recipe of Leonard Bernstein's wife, Felicia Montealegre. I can't believe I remember her name, <u>much less</u> how to spell it, especially given the fact that her recipe was a gluey, milky, disappointing concoction that practically bankrupted me."
—Nora Ephron, *The Most of Nora Ephron* (2013)

"LET ALONE" AND "MUCH LESS"

Nuance Practice*

Magazine writers often use *much less* or *let alone* to hammer home a point. Match the source with the appropriate passage.

Source

A. *The Atlantic*: Alex Tizon, "In the Land of Missing Persons" (2016)

B. *The Bitter Southerner*: Jodi Cash, "Leveling the Field for Family Farms" (2017)

C. *Commentary*: Ben Schachter, "Forgetful Architecture" (2010)

D. *Esquire*: Jessica Pishko, "The FBI Accused Him of Terrorism. He Couldn't Tie His Shoes." (2016)

E. *The Atlantic*: Megan Rose and ProPublica, "The Deal Prosecutors Offer When They Have No Cards Left to Play" (2017)

Passage

1. "'Care of land depends on people who are not in a constant emergency, who know it well and who will take care of it well,' Mary says. 'So, to have that, we've got to have an economy that makes it possible for those people to even exist, much less survive.'"

2. "She and Dolly took turns filling me in. I'd never heard of the Funny River, much less the fire that had ravaged the Kenai. They told me a body had been found, and that its DNA had been tested."

---

* For answers, see page 207 of the Answer Key.

3. "Tony is 51, has high cholesterol, and recently had malignant carcinomas excised from his back and ankle. 'I need my kids prepared for life after Dad,' he says. Peyton couldn't hit a nail with a hammer, <u>let alone</u> brush his teeth or buy groceries. So in the fall of 2014, Tony enrolled him at the E.H. Gentry Facility in Talladega, Alabama, a rehabilitation program for adults with sensory disabilities that focuses on independent living."

4. "Courts only assess guilt or innocence before a conviction. After that, appellate courts focus solely on fairness. Did everyone follow the rules and live up to their duties? Getting a re-hearing of the facts is a monumental, often decades-long quest through a legal thicket. Most defendants never get to start the process, <u>let alone</u> win."

5. "It is hard to design a memorial, <u>let alone</u> a Holocaust museum."

SIXTEEN

"As Diverse As"

People <u>as diverse as</u> James Baldwin and Michelle Obama, Miles Davis and Toni Morrison, Spike Lee and Denzel Washington, and anonymous teachers, store clerks, steelworkers, and physicians, were all products of the Great Migration. They were all children whose life chances were altered because a parent or grandparent had made the hard decision to leave.

—Isabel Wilkerson, *The Warmth of Other Suns: The Epic Story of America's Great Migration* (2010)

Overview

The phrase *as diverse as* is particularly useful when trying to construct an expansive list of examples. Notice the territory covered when it is used by the international relations expert Robin Niblett in a 2016 article in *Foreign Affairs*. He is describing the possible demise of liberalism.

> Large emerging-market democracies, such as Brazil, India, Nigeria, and South Africa, have so far failed to overcome entrenched obstacles to sustainable economic growth and social cohesion. And the perception that U.S. global power is waning and that the Washington consensus does not guarantee economic progress has bolstered strongmen in countries as diverse as the Philippines, Thailand, and Turkey, who have undermined the institutional checks and balances that underpin liberal democracy.

By pointing to a wide range of locales, each distinct from the others, Niblett is able to communicate the alarming scope of the issue he is trying to address.

Yet the utility of *as diverse as* extends beyond geography. In "Lessons from the Front Line of Corporate Nudging," three analysts at the consulting firm McKinsey & Company—Anna Güntner, Konstantin Lucks, and Julia Sperling-Magro—use the phrase to convey the broad reach of their recommendations.

> To span the experiences of customers and employees, teams must pursue initiatives in areas as diverse as in-store service, digital operations, and HR processes.

And in *The Truth About Animals*, the zoologist Lucy Cooke uses it when discussing recent interest in the moral dimensions of wildlife.

"AS DIVERSE AS"

This is a hot topic right now, with researchers like the esteemed primatologist Dr. Frans de Waal pointing out that the basis of morality—a combination of empathy and a sense of fairness—is found in species <u>as diverse as</u> monkeys and rats.

A number of variations of *as diverse as* exist, as you'll see in the Notes section. These include

- *as <u>different</u> as*
- *as <u>disparate</u> as*
- *as <u>varied</u> as*

The variety is fitting. It's kind of nice that the options for *as diverse as* are actually as wide-ranging as the items the phrase is designed to introduce.

Notes

1. **Note how the phrase "as diverse as" can establish wide boundaries for a particular grouping.**

   "Starting in the 1970s, the mainstream environmental movement latched onto a quasi-religious ideology, greenism, which can be found in the manifestoes of activists <u>as diverse as</u> Al Gore, the Unabomber, and Pope Francis."
   —Steven Pinker, *Enlightenment Now: The Case for Reason, Science, Humanism, and Progress* (2018)

   "[Dan] Siroker started a new company, Optimizely, which allows organizations to perform rapid A/B testing. In 2012, Optimizely was used by Obama as well as his opponent, Mitt Romney, to maximize sign-ups, volunteers, and donations. It's also used by companies <u>as diverse as</u> Netflix, TaskRabbit, and *New York* magazine."
   —Seth Stephens-Davidowitz, *Everybody Lies: Big Data, New Data, and What the Internet Can Tell Us About Who We Really Are* (2017)

   "Of all the writers working today, [William] Vollmann must be the most free: He writes fiction, essays, monographs, criticism, memoir, and history, usually merging several forms at once, taking on subjects <u>as diverse as</u> Japanese Noh theater, train hopping, and the Nez Perce War, all the while dilating to whatever length suits him."
   —Nathaniel Rich, "The Most Honest Book About Climate Change Yet" (2018)

2. **Note how "as diverse as" has many variations.**

   "[Gandhi's] prolific writings in that turbulent era inspired thinkers <u>as disparate as</u> W. E. B. Du Bois and Reinhold Niebuhr."
   —Pankaj Mishra, "The Great Protester" (2018)

"About two-thirds of Americans in a recent Pew survey expressed the view that declining trust—in government, in one another—is hampering our ability to confront the country's problems. Yet trust is not gone. It binds the military, as I've seen firsthand in locales <u>as varied as</u> Fallujah and Kandahar, Fort Bragg and Coronado."
—former Secretary of Defense James Mattis, "The Enemy Within" (2019)

"The spaciousness of its too perfectly constructed sets, the subjugation of story and theme to abstract compositional balance, the precision choreography, even—especially—in scenes of violence and chaos, the entire repertoire of colors, angles, fonts, and textures: these were constants in films <u>as wildly different as</u> *Barry Lyndon* (1975) and *The Shining* (1980), *Full Metal Jacket* (1987) and *Eyes Wide Shut* (1999)."
—Dan Chiasson, "*2001: A Space Odyssey*: What It Means, and How It Was Made" (2018)

3. **Note how one of these variations, "as different as," can be especially useful when writing about science.**
"Versions of the same genes sculpt the front-to-back organization of the bodies of creatures <u>as different as</u> flies and mice."
—Neil Shubin, *Your Inner Fish: A Journey into the 3.5-Billion-Year History of the Human Body* (2008)

"Animals <u>as diverse as</u> salamanders, bluebirds, and humans tend to harbor similar communities of bacteria if they live in close quarters."
—Ed Yong, *I Contain Multitudes: The Microbes Within Us and a Grander View of Life* (2016)

NOTES ON NUANCE

Nuance Practice*

(1) We've noted that the phrase *as diverse as* can helpfully introduce a list of vastly different countries. What's interesting about the three examples below is that they all reference a certain small Eastern European country. It's apparently a popular choice when you want your list to include an eclectic set of locales.

> The Institute has a long history of alumni who become English Language Fellows; in fact, since 2006, 32 alumni have served as [fellows] around the world in countries <u>as diverse as</u> _____, Rwanda, Thailand, and Brazil.
> —Website for Middlebury College's Institute for International Studies

> Discussions of the "ideological" function of orthography have included analyses of orthographic activism and politics in Galicia, the scholarly transcription of African-American English, and "postcolonial orthographies" that have arisen in countries <u>as diverse as</u> _____, Haiti, Malaysia and Indonesia.
> —Jennifer Bann and John Corbett, *Spelling Scots: The Orthography of Literary Scots, 1700–2000* (2015)

> Every week correspondents, journalists and writers from around the world report on the stories behind the headlines, often bringing a personal perspective to them. There are few countries and subjects which have not featured on the program—places <u>as diverse as</u> the Faroes, _____ in Eastern Europe, the

---

* For answers, see page 208 of the Answer Key.

Himalayan kingdom of Bhutan and one of Africa's smallest countries—Sao Tome and Principe.
—Website for the "From Our Correspondents" series on BBC Radio 4

Fill in these missing letters to discover the name of the country.

M _ L _ _ _ A

(2) In his 2016 memoir, one of the more famous rock musicians of all time uses *as varied as* to describe the many minor run-ins with the law he had while growing up in New Jersey.

> I'd managed to be hauled into local police stations for hard-core crimes <u>as varied as</u> not purchasing a beach badge, hitchhiking and getting caught in my girlfriend's father's "borrowed" Cadillac.

Name the musician.

First Name: _____
Last Name: _____

(<u>Hint</u>: The title of his memoir is *Born to Run*, which is also the title of one of his most famous albums and songs.)

Nuance Review: "As Diverse As" ↔ "To"

You might have noticed a similarity between the phrase *as diverse as* in this chapter and the word *to* from back in chapter 9. Both can introduce a wide range of content. Here are a couple of examples of how you might exchange one move for the other, particularly if you have already used one of them in a nearby paragraph or section.

I. "As Diverse As" → "To"

Original: "The emotional support spouses provide has numerous biological and psychological benefits. Being near a familiar person—even an acquaintance, let alone a spouse—can have effects <u>as diverse as</u> lowering heart rate, improving immune function, and reducing depression."

—Nicholas Christakis and James Fowler, *Connected: The Surprising Power of Our Social Networks and How They Shape Our Lives* (2009)

Possible Exchange: "The emotional support spouses provide has numerous biological and psychological benefits. Being near a familiar person—even an acquaintance, let alone a spouse—can have effects ranging from lowering heart rate, <u>to</u> improving immune function, <u>to</u> reducing depression."

II. "To" → "As Diverse As"

Original: "I was ready for my close-up as Black Super-Art DJ, starting in the present, then shattering time and place as I stepped back through the past, working in everything from seventies rock and soul <u>to</u> Mingus <u>to</u> Les McCann <u>to</u> show tunes <u>to</u> jazz standards <u>to</u> classic disco."

—Questlove, *Creative Quest* (2018)

Possible Exchange: "I was ready for my close-up as Black Super-Art DJ, starting in the present, then shattering time and place as I stepped back through the past, working in music <u>as diverse as</u> seventies rock, soul, Mingus, Les McCann, show tunes, jazz standards, and classic disco."

SEVENTEEN

"More ____ Than ____"

On December 16, in an icy, drenching rain, Frederick led thirty-two thousand soldiers across the Silesian frontier. He met practically no resistance; the campaign was <u>more</u> an occupation <u>than</u> an invasion.

—Robert K. Massie, *Catherine the Great: Portrait of a Woman* (2011)

But given that there are in effect no limits on the admission of hearsay evidence—the only requirement is that the tribunal deem the evidence "relevant and helpful"—the detainee's opportunity to question witnesses is likely to be <u>more</u> theoretical <u>than</u> real.

—Justice Anthony Kennedy, *Boumediene v. Bush* (2008)

Overview

Sometimes it can be good to communicate descriptions using two reference points, especially if each helps give contrasting shape to the other. The surgeon and *New Yorker* staff writer Atul Gawande does this nicely in *Being Mortal*, a book that intermingles general reflections about end-of-life medical choices with personal stories about how hard it is to make those kind of choices with and for family members.

In one chapter, Gawande profiles Bill Thomas, a physician who spent his post–medical school years splitting time between shifts in the emergency room and tending to the cattle, horses, and chickens he and his wife raised on their farm in Upstate New York. "[Bill] was at that point," Gawande explains, "<u>more</u> farmer <u>than</u> doctor."

See how pairing *farmer* with *doctor* establishes a useful dichotomy? Bill is closer to the farmer side of the spectrum, Gawande suggests, than he is to the doctor side. The *more* ____ *than* ____ move makes that calibration possible.

A somewhat more conspicuous example comes in the short story "Chaunt" by Joy Williams. She places one *more* ____ *than* ____ move right after another *more* ____ *than* ____ move in a way that makes both moves stand out.

> Nor would she be able to state with any surety whether it was Billy who had discovered the church at Chaunt or whether the boys had discovered it together. It had been <u>more</u> chapel <u>than</u> church, with a single long rectangular room. And <u>more</u> rubble <u>than</u> chapel now.

Simply saying "It had resembled a chapel" or "It was rubble now" wouldn't have conveyed the same meaning. But by using *more* ____ *than* ____, Williams gives herself—and her readers—the opportunity for subtlety and gradation. You'll see additional examples of that in the Notes section.

"MORE ___ THAN ___"

Notes

1. **Note how "more ___ than ___" can calibrate a description, shading meaning toward one quality instead of another.**
"He sinks his fingers through the gray roots of her hair and holds her face there. It's a strange gesture, <u>more</u> gruff <u>than</u> romantic, his little unconscious parody of how she feels towards him, maybe—it makes her think, of all things, of a mother bear cuffing its cub."
—Karen Russell, "The New Veterans" (2013)

"To preserve that very high standard, firing people was also necessary, and not just a few: 'I do all of the firing. At times, I've fired maybe one out of every three people I've hired. That might make people think I'm bad at hiring, but I think I'm quite good at hiring.' This sounded tough, and doubtless it was meant to. But Paul in action was <u>more</u> humanist <u>than</u> tyrant. According to one of his assistants from Kayak's early days, he once threw up in the bathroom the morning before a firing. He still offered to meet with each fired person outside of work."
—Tracy Kidder, *A Truck Full of Money* (2016)

2. **Note how "more ___ than ___" is a good technique for adding precision to the way someone reacted.**
"Although a doctor in the article called the outbreak 'rather devastating,' I was <u>more</u> annoyed <u>than</u> alarmed by the news."
—David France, *How to Survive a Plague: The Inside Story of How Citizens and Science Tamed AIDS* (2016)

"'Why are you so late? Your mother was worried about you.' My father sounded <u>more</u> annoyed <u>than</u> concerned."
—Bernhard Schlink, *The Reader* (1995)

3. **Note how "more ___ than ___" is often used with adjectives.**
   "It was a seamless, privileged life—until it fell apart. In 1918 Eleanor [Roosevelt] discovered her husband's affair with her social secretary, Lucy Mercer. That revelation traumatized her and permanently transformed their marriage, which became <u>more</u> collaborative <u>than</u> intimate."
   —Susan Dunn, "Eleanor in War and Love" (2016)

   "Some critics asserted that [Governor George Romney's] stance was <u>more</u> political <u>than</u> moral, just as some believed that his push for small cars was as much a matter of pragmatic necessity as environment-conscious philosophy."
   —David Maraniss, *Once in a Great City: A Detroit Story* (2015)

4. **Note how "more ___ than ___" can, on occasion, be used with nouns—in an adjective kind of way.**
   "Suddenly, genes from organisms that would never have been able to mate in nature could be combined in the laboratory. But those initial tools were <u>more</u> hatchet <u>than</u> scalpel, and, because they could recognize only short stretches within the vast universe of the human genome, the editing was rarely precise."
   —Michael Specter, "The Gene Hackers" (2015)

5. **Note how "more than" can also be used with nouns in a nonadjective kind of way.**
   "During the summer of the campaign, the siege of the legations at Peking by the Boxers and the American share in the relief expedition pointed up the far-flung role the country was now playing. Its most convinced and vocal champion was [President William] McKinley's new vice-presidential nominee, Theodore Roosevelt, who took the President's place as chief campaigner. Unsure of victory, for 'full dinner pail' was <u>more</u> a slogan <u>than</u> a

fact, he campaigned so vigorously and indefatigably that to the public and cartoonists the Rough Rider with the teeth, pince-nez, and unquenchable zest appeared to be the real candidate."
—Barbara Tuchman, *The Proud Tower: A Portrait of the World before the War, 1890–1914* (1966)

NOTES ON NUANCE

Nuance Practice*

(1) **Alliteration:** Sometimes writers add a further dimension to their use of *more ___ than ___* by including a bit of alliteration. See if you can find the right word to complete the alliterative pairing in the examples below.

- The first example comes from *A Beautiful Mind*, Sylvia Nasar's biography of the mathematician John Nash, who won the Nobel Prize in Economics in 1994 and would later be portrayed by Russell Crowe in the Oscar-winning film.

    > By election day in early November, Eleanor strongly suspected that she was pregnant. On Thanksgiving, when she invited Nash to come to her place, she was absolutely certain, having missed a second period by then. Nash seemed, oddly enough, <u>more</u> _____ <u>than</u> panicked.

    (A) pretentious
    (B) pleased
    (C) putrid
    (D) petrified

- Nobel Prize winners also figure in this next example, which is taken from the book *The 4% Universe: Dark Matter, Dark Energy, and the Race to Discover the Rest of Reality* by Richard Panek. The book offers a compelling account of the breakthrough research that earned Saul Perlmutter, Brian P. Schmidt, and Adam G. Riess the 2011 Nobel Prize in Physics.

---

* For answers, see page 208 of the Answer Key.

"MORE ___ THAN ___"

Cosmology was where old astronomers went to die. It was <u>more</u> philosophy <u>than</u> _____.

(A) physics
(B) philology
(C) philately
(D) phonography

(2) **Proper Names:** Proper names can also add an extra punch to the *more* ___ *than* ___ construction. The name in the blank below belongs to a twentieth-century painter who created magazine covers for the *Saturday Evening Post* for more than fifty years. One of his most famous images is of six-year-old Ruby Bridges, who was the first African American child to desegregate William Frantz Elementary School back in 1960.

> By the 1970s, my father's cinematic productions of American domesticity—the home movies of our first family Christmas, our first Easter, our first strained family visit to the Florida Keys to visit my mother's disapproving parents—had declined into sporadic snapshots <u>more</u> Diane Arbus <u>than</u> _____.
> —Susan Faludi, *In the Darkroom* (2016)

(A) Andy Warhol
(B) Norman Rockwell
(C) Frida Kahlo
(D) Georgia O'Keeffe

(3) **Alliteration and Proper Names:** Sometimes writers will even make use of alliteration and proper names at the same time. The following example appeared in the magazine *Wired*. It describes the company Essential, which aims to create simple, beautifully designed smartphones.

> There's no branding on the devices themselves. Essential aspires to be <u>more</u> Armani <u>than</u> _____: understated, confident, cool, in a way that doesn't need logos.

(A) Abercrombie
(B) American Airlines
(C) Applebee's
(D) Airbnb

EIGHTEEN

"Less ____ Than ____" and "Less Than"

> *It is <u>less</u> a driveway <u>than</u> a road—but also a portion of road that is shared by both neighbors and nobody else, owing to how it cuts right through one man's property and ends at the other man's, which occupies the westernmost tip of the island.*
>
> —Eric Konigsberg, "The Billionaire Battle in the Bahamas" (2015)

> *Henry Pearson had the reputation of being <u>less than</u> supportive of the advancement of female employees.*
>
> —Margot Lee Shetterly, *Hidden Figures: The American Dream and the Untold Story of the Black Women Mathematicians Who Helped Win the Space Race* (2016)

Overview

Like *more* ____ *than* ____, the construction *less* ____ *than* ____ gives you a way to describe something through a subtle distinction. You start by distancing your description from one reference point, and then you push it toward something a bit more accurate. Allie Rowbottom uses this tactic in *Jell-O Girls*, her memoir about growing up in the family that turned a somewhat obscure substance called gelatin into an iconic household brand.

> Long before Jell-O crossed oceans and landed in LeRoy, it was known just as gelatin, a product confined to the kitchens of European royalty, <u>less</u> a convenience product <u>than</u> a luxury.

See what that *less* ____ *than* ____ comparison does? See how it places gelatin along a useful continuum?

The British writer Tessa Hadley does something similar in "The Bunty Club," a short story that, like Rowbottom's memoir, focuses on family relationships. Hadley, however, signals the start of her continuum not with a comma but with the aid of a dash. The extra dose of punctuation helps emphasize the comparison.

> In the years since their father died, their mother, Evelyn, hadn't changed anything in these rooms—<u>less</u> out of respect <u>than</u> out of indifference.

The historian Ron Chernow, whose biography of Alexander Hamilton inspired the hit Broadway musical by Lin-Manuel Miranda, takes a slightly different approach in one of his earlier books, *The House of Morgan: An American Banking Dynasty and the Rise of Modern Finance*, which won the National Book Award back in 1991. Instead of writing *less* ____ *than* ____, he goes with *less* ____ *and more* ____.

> Although the Morgan bank took stakes in its companies, partners agreed in the 1920s not to get involved in outside

> enterprises. Gradually, if imperceptibly, the banker was becoming <u>less</u> a corporate partner <u>and more</u> a professional, a disinterested intermediary.

The difference in wording is minor. The overall structure and effect remain the same.

Something else is worth mentioning. It's important to distinguish *less* ____ *than* ____ from *less than* _____. You can use *less* ___ *than* ____ to shift your audience away from one reference point and toward another. But you can use *less than* ____ for a different purpose: to signal that something has fallen short of a certain standard. Two examples show how this works.

The first comes from *The Poison Squad: One Chemist's Single-Minded Crusade for Food Safety at the Turn of the Twentieth Century* by Deborah Blum, who is the director of the Knight Science Journalism program at MIT.

> The hearings led to the Butter Act of 1886, which passed with support from both parties and was signed by President Cleveland. But thanks to intervention from the meatpackers, the law was <u>less than</u> hard-hitting, imposing a tax of merely two cents a pound on margarine, leaving the imitation still cheaper to produce than the real thing.

The second comes from *Circe* by Madeline Miller, who specializes in adapting classical myths into novels for modern audiences. (Her first book, *The Song of Achilles*, won the Orange Prize for Fiction in 2012 and was a *New York Times* best seller.)

> Her hair is streaked like a lynx. And her chin. There is a sharpness to it that is <u>less than</u> pleasing.

You'll see instances of both *less* _____ *than* _____ and *less than* ____ in the Notes section of this chapter. Each uses a helpful amount of indirection to ultimately arrive at an appealing form of description.

Notes

1. **Note how "less ___ than ___" functions very much like the move from the previous chapter: "more ___ than ___." Only now the shift is in the opposite direction.**

"He seemed <u>less</u> angry <u>than</u> curious, but it was an accusation just the same."

—Richard Russo, *Bridge of Sighs* (2007)

"At the beginning of the 20th century, civil libertarians in America worried most about the danger of the government silencing political speech: think of Eugene V. Debs, the socialist candidate for president, who was imprisoned in 1919 for publicly protesting American involvement during World War I. But by the late 1960s, after the Supreme Court started to protect unpopular speakers more consistently, some critics worried that free speech in America was threatened <u>less</u> by government suppression <u>than</u> by editorial decisions made by the handful of private mass-media corporations like NBC and CBS that disproportionately controlled public discourse."

—Jeffrey Rosen, "Google's Gatekeepers" (2008)

2. **Note how "less ___ than ___" can work nicely at the end of a sentence.**

"Even the mother he carried inside him was <u>less</u> a memory <u>than</u> a dream."

—Garth Risk Hallberg, *City on Fire* (2015)

"Frederick absolutely hated Hugh Auld's 'right of the robber' in taking the slave's earnings. Here Frederick was again, now twenty years old, treated as a boy serving the ends of white people who still owned his body and his labor. His troubles, he maintained, as ever, were '<u>less</u> physical <u>than</u> mental.'"

—David Blight, *Frederick Douglass: Prophet of Freedom* (2018)

"LESS ___ THAN ___" AND "LESS THAN"

3. **Note how you can put a couple of options between "less ___ than ___."**
"More than two decades after his death, in the Summer 1986 issue of *The American Scholar*, a one-time student of [Randall] Jarrell's, reviewing a collection of the poet's letters, made the review <u>less</u> a literary or biographical appraisal <u>than</u> an occasion for continuing to try to exorcise the vile phantom of suicide."
—William Styron, *Darkness Visible* (1989)

4. **Note how a variant of "less ___ than ___" is "less than ___." Rather than set up two reference points, this slightly different construction relies on just one.**
"The arrangement was <u>less than</u> smooth. Things like waking up in the morning to find those familiar dirty dishes in the sink were particularly vexing. It was no problem for me to slip into the dismaying role of the ticked-off, hectoring dad."
—Mark Jacobson, "65" (2014)

"I don't eat mussels in restaurants unless I know the chef personally, or have seen, with my own eyes, how they store and hold their mussels for service. I love mussels. But in my experience, most cooks are <u>less than</u> scrupulous in their handling of them."
—Anthony Bourdain, *Kitchen Confidential* (2000)

"[Ambrose Ransom] Wright was 'a very gifted man, a powerful writer, an effective orator, and a rare lawyer.' He was notorious for possessing a bullwhip temper which made him 'self-willed and combative.' Like his division commander, Wright had been <u>less than</u> enthusiastic about secession."
—Allen Guelzo, *Gettysburg* (2013)

NOTES ON NUANCE

Nuance Practice: "Less __ Than __"*

(1) In *Hero of the Empire: The Boer War, a Daring Escape, and the Making of Winston Churchill*, Candice Millard recounts the adventures and accomplishments of Winston Churchill, back when he was a twenty-four-year-old journalist covering the Boer War in South Africa. Early on in the book, Millard offers a sense of Churchill's grand ambitions and capacity for self-promotion. She uses the *less* _____ *than* _____ move to stress how un-English these qualities were, aligning Churchill instead with the American presidential family to which he would later become a major World War II ally.

> For a member of Churchill's high social class, such bold, unabashed ambition was a novelty, if not an outright scandal. He had been born a British aristocrat, a direct descendant of John Churchill, the 1st Duke of Marlborough, his parents personal friends of the Prince of Wales, Queen Victoria's oldest son and heir. Yet in his open pursuit of fame and popular favor, Churchill seemed far <u>less</u> Victorian <u>than</u> _____. "The immortal [P. T.] Barnum himself had not a greater gift for making himself and his affairs the talk of the world," his first biographer, Alexander MacCallum Scott, would write just a few years later. "Winston advertises himself as simply and unconsciously as he breathes."

---

* For answers, see page 208 of the Answer Key.

"LESS ___ THAN ___" AND "LESS THAN"

Fill in the blank with the family name Millard turned into an adjective.

(A) Wilsonian
(B) Jeffersonian
(C) Madisonian
(D) Rooseveltian

(2) In February 1946, the American diplomat George Kennan sent what has come to be known as the "Long Telegram" from his post at the US Embassy in Moscow. Considered one of the most important documents of the Cold War, it helped establish the strategy that came to be known as "containment." The penultimate paragraph contains a tidy use of *less _____ than _____*.

> We must formulate and put forward for other nations a much more positive and constructive picture of the sort of world we would like to see than we have put forward in past. It is not enough to urge people to develop political processes similar to our own. Many foreign peoples, in Europe at least, are tired and frightened by experiences of past, and are <u>less</u> interested in abstract freedom <u>than</u> in **s _ c _ _ i _ y**. They are seeking guidance rather than responsibilities. We should be better able than Russians to give them this. And unless we do, Russians certainly will.

Fill in the missing letters: **s _ c _ _ i _ y**

Nuance Practice: "Less Than ___"*

The Japanese writer Haruki Murakami appears to be a big fan of using the variant of *less* ____ *than* ____ that we mentioned, the one that puts the two words together without any break between the *less* and the *than*.

> It was no mystery why so many women in this world might find him charming (to the same degree they might find me <u>less than</u> desirable).
> —*Killing Commendatore* (2017)

> Their relationship had become <u>less than</u> ideal with the passage of time, and now they seemed to fight about the stupidest things whenever they met.
> —*Blind Willow, Sleeping Woman* (2006)

Each of the following examples comes from one of Murakami's short stories. The first two are from "Samsa in Love," which was published in the *New Yorker* in 2013. The second two are from the collection *Men without Women*, which appeared in Japanese in 2014 and in English in 2017. Match the phrases in the Word Bank with the sentence they complete.

Word Bank: complimentary, satisfying, clean, thrilled

"The room was as it had been before: only a bed with a bare mattress that was <u>less than</u> _____."

"Yet the woman seemed to find his answer <u>less than</u> _____."

"They were oblivious to the gasps and slammed brakes that accompanied their sudden and daring lane changes, and to the <u>less-than</u>-_____ words directed at them by their fellow drivers."

"Thus when Oba, who ran the garage where he serviced his car, recommended a young woman to be his personal driver, Kafuku looked <u>less than</u> _____."

---

* For answers, see page 208 of the Answer Key.

NINETEEN
Nuance Spotlight

WILLIAM F. BUCKLEY JR.
(1925–2008)

America has lost one of its finest writers and thinkers. [William F.] Buckley was one of the great founders of the modern conservative movement. He brought conservative thought into the political mainstream and helped lay the intellectual foundation for America's victory in the Cold War and for the conservative movement that continues to this day.
—President George W. Bush (2008)

Overview

We've now come to our third chance to do a "Nuance Spotlight," where instead of learning a new move, we look at a writer who uses a wide range of them. The first spotlight was on Jane Austen. The second was on James Baldwin. This one will be on William F. Buckley Jr., the founder and longtime editor of the magazine the *National Review* as well as the author of over forty books.

Here's how the business journalist and editor Marshall Loeb described Buckley's talent and influence shortly after Buckley's death in 2008: "Even if you disagreed sharply with [Buckley's] positions, you knew that you had to do your homework before you took him on in any kind of debate. He was a font of wisdom, and he knew how to wield the language like a knight's sword."

Loeb was referring to Buckley's dazzling speaking skills, but he could just have easily been referring to Buckley's dazzling writing skills—not the least of which was his ability to be at once both precise and productive. As Loeb explains early on in his remembrance, Buckley "was a writer for whom the word 'prolific' might have been invented." He wrote about politics. He wrote about religion. He wrote about travel, airplanes, and higher education. He even wrote several novels, including a set of spy thrillers centered around the fictional CIA character Blackford Oakes.

In the first Blackford Oakes novel, *Saving the Queen*, which was published in 1976, Buckley makes frequent use of the *at once* move. "Blackford was <u>at once</u> relieved, intrigued, and enraged," he writes toward the beginning of the story. He later returns to the move three separate times, even combining it with the *however* move at one point.

- "Alistair looked <u>at once</u> disappointed and patient."
- "'Hear, hear!' the boys said, <u>at once</u> docile and chauvinistic."

NUANCE SPOTLIGHT

- "Alice's parents were <u>at once</u> relieved that Alice had got rid of Tom Oakes and distressed that Carol had fallen prey to someone who, <u>however</u> dashing and handsome, was manifestly irresponsible."

You'll see in the examples below, however, that the *at once* move is by no means the only bit of nuance Buckley employs. Range is one of his many rhetorical virtues.

Notes

1. Almost

"But there was a nice rhetorical resonance and an intrinsic, <u>almost</u> nonchalant suggestion of an exciting symbiosis."
—William F. Buckley Jr., *God and Man at Yale* (1951)

2. Even

"It is not an unimportant historical point that the Inquisition was a state policy (1479–1820), done, to be sure, with ecclesial collusion. But when it was abandoned, this came about not so much at the prompting of a Church set on reform as at the prompting of a civilized world progressively indignant, <u>even</u> revolted by, practices which, finally, the Catholic Church abandoned."
—William F. Buckley Jr., *Nearer, My God: An Autobiography of Faith* (1997)

3. If Not

"To be sure, a great nation can indulge its little extravagances, as I have repeatedly stressed; but a long enough series of little extravagances, as I have also said, can add up to a stagnating <u>if not</u> a crippling economic overhead."
—William F. Buckley Jr., *Up from Liberalism* (1959)

4. To

"It worked, and in a few months the nuns learned that Florida Huerta was badly underinstructed but extraordinarily gifted. It was only a matter of weeks before she caught up with other girls her own age. Her behavior was exemplary. She studied and read six hours every day and did chores for four hours, everything from cleaning toilets <u>to</u> teaching the little girls how to read."
—William F. Buckley Jr., *Brothers No More* (1995)

5. **Let Alone**

"I don't yet know whether I—<u>let alone</u> the world of letters—am indebted to Mr. Samuel Vaughan of Doubleday for his mischievous suggestion that I write a novel in the first place; but I am certainly indebted to him, and to his associates, Betty Prashker and Hugh O'Neill, for their acute criticisms and fine suggestions."

—William F. Buckley Jr., *Saving the Queen* (1976)

TWENTY

"Without Being" and "Without"

> *Chief Justice Roberts, it soon became evident, was a brilliant writer—clear, epigrammatic, eloquent <u>without being</u> verbose.*
> —Jeffrey Toobin, *The Oath: The Obama White House and the Supreme Court* (2012)

> *Henry now understood the taxidermist's keen interest in the Flaubert story: Julian slaughters quantities of innocent animals, but it doesn't affect his salvation. The story offers redemption <u>without</u> remorse.*
> —Yann Martel, *Beatrice and Virgil* (2010)

Overview

Several moves in this book have focused on how to communicate gradation. Take, for instance, the move in chapter 2 involving the word *almost*. We learned that you can use it to show descriptive steps along a continuum. A helpful example comes in *The Mysterious Affair at Styles* by the queen of detective stories, Agatha Christie. When Christie notes that one of the characters shakes hands "with a hearty, almost painful, grip," we understand the progression she has established: the handshake is so hearty that it borders on being painful. The *almost* tells us that we haven't quite reached the point of painfulness yet, but we're close.

Something similar happens with the moves in this chapter: *without being* and *without*. By creating definitional contours between the words they neighbor, each helps better delineate the targeted quality.

We can begin to see how this works if we look at another example from the world of detective fiction, this time in the form of a comment about the author who pioneered the genre, Edgar Allan Poe. "[Poe] was remarkable for self-respect, without haughtiness," reads a letter describing Poe during his school days.

See how the *without* in that sentence establishes a relationship between self-respect and haughtiness? See how it implies that self-respect can eventually rise to the level of haughtiness or at least be contaminated by elements *of* haughtiness?

What makes Poe remarkable, the sentence is saying, is that his self-respect remained a safe distance away from all that. Intact and unspoiled, this quality of his doesn't have any hint of haughtiness.

The mechanics of the move become clearer, I think, when writers use the phrase *without being* instead of just *without*. A theater critic once praised Poe's mother, the English-born actress Elizabeth Arnold Hopkins Poe, by observing that "it is difficult to be sprightly

<u>without being</u> fantastic, and to act the hoyden* <u>without being</u> gross and mawkish" but that "Mrs. Poe has hit the happy medium." And the move pops up again in a book about Benjamin Franklin by the English professor Alfred Owen Aldridge, for whom the A. Owen Aldridge Prize in Comparative Literature is named. Here's how Aldridge describes the impression Franklin made in Paris during his time as an ambassador to France.

> His eyes were shadowed by large glasses and in his hand he carried a white cane. He spoke little. He knew how to be impolite <u>without being</u> rude, and his pride seemed to be that of nature. Such a person was made to excite the curiosity of Paris.

Sure, Franklin may have lacked a certain amount of grace and refinement at times. But he didn't intentionally disrespect people. The use of *without being* highlights that distinction.

Additional distinctions appear in the Notes section. I think all of them, as I said, are slightly easier to grasp when the author uses *without being* instead of just *without*. But both moves are certainly worth trying.

---

* The Merriam-Webster dictionary defines a *hoyden* as "a girl or woman of saucy, boisterous, or carefree behavior."

Notes

1. **Note how "without being" can be used to signal a welcome form of restraint.**
   "Refreshingly in the world of strident foodies, [Sweetgreen cofounder Nic] Jammet and his colleagues manage to be ambitious <u>without being</u> sanctimonious."
   —Michael Specter, "Freedom from Fries" (2015)

   "The dinner itself . . . was delicious <u>without being</u> grandiose."
   —David Foster Wallace, *Infinite Jest* (1996)

2. **Note how following one "without being" with another "without being" can create a nice rhythm.**
   "Julie Kikuchi is thirty-six. She looks twenty-six. She is short <u>without being</u> small. She is irreverent <u>without being</u> crude."
   —Jeffrey Eugenides, *Middlesex* (2002)

   "I stand here today for her family—which is my family—and for my family and all the other families in the world who would want to be here, but could not be here. I have beside me up here millions of people who are living and standing straight and erect, and knowing something about dignity <u>without being</u> cold and aloof, knowing something about being contained <u>without being</u> unapproachable—people who have learned something from Coretta Scott King."
   —Maya Angelou, "Eulogy for Coretta Scott King" (2006)

3. **Note how the word that accompanies "without" doesn't have to be "being."**
   "The difficulty with Densher was that he looked vague <u>without</u> looking weak—idle <u>without</u> looking empty."
   —Henry James, *The Wings of the Dove* (1902)

"WITHOUT BEING" AND "WITHOUT"

4. **Note how no word actually has to accompany "without." It can operate alone.**

"Like Mr. Kurtz in Conrad's *Heart of Darkness*, they were 'hollow to the core,' 'reckless <u>without</u> hardihood, greedy <u>without</u> audacity and cruel <u>without</u> courage.' They believed in nothing and 'could get (themselves) to believe anything—anything.'"

—Hannah Arendt, *The Origins of Totalitarianism* (1951)

NOTES ON NUANCE

Nuance Practice*

(1) Chronicling the energy, greed, and excess of New York in the late twentieth century, the novel *The Bonfire of the Vanities* by Tom Wolfe was a publishing sensation when it first came out in 1987. Its success was so meteoric that after being released in twenty-seven installments in *Rolling Stone*, it quickly topped the best sellers list and became one of those rare books that defined an era. See if you can figure out the missing word in the following description of one of its characters, Reverend Reginald Bacon. It shows how you might use *without being* in a slightly different way.

> There wasn't a trace of emotion on his face. He was one of those thin, rawboned men who look powerful without being _____.

(A) mushy
(B) muscular
(C) monumental
(D) messy

(2) Jane Smiley won the Pulitzer Prize in Fiction in 1992 for *A Thousand Acres*, a novel that reimagines Shakespeare's *King Lear* through the lens of a wealthy farming family in Iowa. Smiley has written several other novels as well, including *Private Life* in 2010, which includes the following use of *without being* in a letter that the main character, Margaret Mayfield, discovers.

> No, the girl is not educated nor evidently intelligent, _____ without being mysterious (though I think there is more to her than meets the eye), but what do you want in a wife at your age?

---

* For answers, see page 209 of the Answer Key.

"WITHOUT BEING" AND "WITHOUT"

Try to guess the word that comes before *without being*.

(A) querulous
(B) quaint
(C) quiet
(D) quixotic

(3) Music critic and record producer Jon Landau is often credited with helping launch the career of Bruce Springsteen. "I saw rock and roll future," Landau wrote back in 1974, "and its name is Bruce Springsteen." Two years later, Landau offered his opinion of another rock legend, Mick Jagger. Reviewing the Rolling Stones album *Sticky Fingers*, Landau wrote that "Jagger's vocal is clearly audible for the first time on the album and I don't care for it. It is mannered, striving for intensity <u>without being</u> wholly _____."

(A) cacophonous
(B) crackling
(C) convincing
(D) creepy

TWENTY-ONE

"All But"

In the glow of their lights, they <u>all but</u> sprang along the aisles in teams of two, swiftly thrusting their hoes up onto the shelves and scraping some of the mess into their tubs.

—Alex Haley, *Roots: The Saga of an American Family* (1976)

The end of August is always a slow time in markets, but this August, trading in bond markets <u>all but</u> vanished.

—Roger Lowenstein, *When Genius Failed: The Rise and Fall of Long-Term Capital Management* (2000)

Overview

The phrase *all but* has an interesting combination of qualities. Consider, for example, the following sentence from a magazine profile of Constance Wu, one of the stars of the 2018 hit movie *Crazy Rich Asians*.

> The mid-July sun at Waialua, on the north shore of Oahu, was already so unforgiving at 9 A.M. that the ice in a cooler of LaCroix near the foot of Constance Wu's chair had <u>all but</u> melted; an assistant heaped up the few remaining cubes around the cans.

The author of the profile, the journalist Jianying Zha, enlists the help of the word *melted* to describe the condition of the ice next to Wu's chair, even though using that word is a bit of a stretch. The ice didn't melt. Or at least it didn't fully melt—some cubes remained around the cans.

By using *all but*, however, Zha can evoke the process of melting while also being careful not to overclaim. The phrase provides her with a helpful mix of reach and restraint. And although on some level it's simply the equivalent of writing that the ice *nearly melted, just about melted, essentially melted,* or *for all practical purposes melted*, there is a compelling compactness to *all but melted* that those substitutes lack.

When you move on to the Notes section, you'll have a chance to see more of what *all but* can do. It's a sturdy, stylish way to express everything from excitement, to despair, to regret.

"ALL BUT"

Notes

1. **Note how "all but" can be used to express excitement.**
   "Cindy had <u>all but</u> sprinted out of the car to get to him, to hug him and stroke his cheeks and give him three kisses."
   —Imbolo Mbue, *Behold the Dreamers* (2016)

   "Ken is a good speaker, even charismatic, as close as you can get to a godless preacher. He has a booming voice, he slaps the palm of his hand to punctuate a point, he <u>all but</u> says amen."
   —A. J. Jacobs, *The Year of Living Biblically* (2007)

2. **Note how "all but" can be used to express despair.**
   "On Thursday after lunch they were again out together. It had become so much a habit that the walk repeated itself without an effort. It had been part of Mabel's scheme that it should be so. During all this morning she had been thinking of her scheme. It was <u>all but</u> hopeless."
   —Anthony Trollope, *The Duke's Children* (1879)

   "It seems she'd been managing very well alone until last year, when everything started failing at once. From an energetic swimmer and gardener and crack crossword puzzle solver she's become <u>all but</u> helpless."
   —Sigrid Nunez, *The Friend* (2018)

3. **Note how "all but" can emphasize loss or defeat.**
   "But just as modern street lighting has slowly blotted the stars from the visible skies, so too have cars and planes and factories and flickering digital screens combined to rob us of a silence that was previously regarded as integral to the health of the human imagination. This changes us. It slowly

removes—without our even noticing it—the very spaces where we can gain a footing in our minds and souls that is not captive to constant pressures or desires or duties. And the smartphone has all but banished them."

  —Andrew Sullivan, "I Used to Be a Human Being" (2016)

"The real estate these schools sat on was valuable, and the feminist movement all but obliterated demand for their offerings, as the domestic talents once suggestive of elegance and good breeding began to look more like instruments of oppression."

  —Alice Gregory, "Lessons from the Last Swiss Finishing School" (2018)

4. Note how "all but" often precedes the word "forgotten" or "impossible."

"One afternoon before a home game, Kennedy approached [Ricky] Henderson at the ballpark and asked if he would teach the other players the art of stealing. Kennedy knew that, in recent years, base stealing had been all but forgotten in the major leagues."

  —David Grann, "Stealing Time" (2005)

"Briggs and Myers were a mother-and-daughter team. To call them 'mildly eccentric' would be indulging in a gender stereotype, but it seems fair to say that they were a little O.C.D. They devoted their lives to their system, and they kept the faith for a very long time. If they had not, there would be no [Myers-Briggs Type Indicator] today.

  "The mother, Katharine Cook Briggs, was born in 1875. When she died, in 1968, the test she inspired was all but forgotten. The daughter, Isabel Briggs Myers, was born in 1897. She codified her mother's method of categorizing personalities, copyrighted it (in 1943), and spent the rest of her life trying to find a permanent home for the product. She died in 1980, just as the test's popularity was taking off."

—Louis Menand, "What Personality Tests Really Deliver" (2018)

"Three months after the first fires had started in Yellowstone, the damage to America's foremost national park was devastating. More than 1.3 million acres of the greater Yellowstone ecosystem, and 36 percent of the park, had burned. Visitors encountered black mountainsides. More than 2 million tons of particulate and 4.4 million tons of carbon monoxide had been released into the air. In some places it was so dark during the day that photography was all but impossible."

—Bharat Anand, *The Content Trap: A Strategist's Guide to Digital Change* (2016)

"He has had to work in all-but-impossible situations—for example, in restricted military areas where he was opposed by bureaucrats, and in the most remote parts of Mongolia and Bhutan, where cultural differences can make research very difficult."

—Tim Flannery, "The Big Melt" (2018)

NOTES ON NUANCE

Nuance Practice*

(1) The Yale historian David Blight published a highly acclaimed biography of Frederick Douglass in 2018. Critics praised the book both for the depth of its research and for the power and grace of its sentences. "It is a work not only of stunning scholarship," raved James McPherson, whose civil war history *Battle Cry of Freedom* won the Pulitzer Prize in 1989, "but also of literary artistry."

Blight uses *all but* throughout the biography to help get his point across. Three examples of that are below. Use the word bank to complete each sentence.

Word Bank: ran, forever, adopted

"Douglass was and is a hero; he has been <u>all but</u> _____ as a national figure in Ireland, Scotland, and Britain. His *Narrative* is read all over the world."

"A delegation of friends gathered at the docks to meet him. But so anxious was Douglass to see his family, he <u>all but</u> ____ to the train that took him to Lynn within a half hour."

"Perhaps the thing in life he needed most was <u>all but</u> ____ beyond his grasp, and certainly not achievable in one woman. Douglass might cling to some of the female relationships in his life at the same time any profoundly deep love may have been an unbearable intensity."

---

* For answers, see page 209 of the Answer Key.

(2) Douglass himself uses *all but* in one of his own books, *My Bondage and My Freedom*, a piece of writing Blight calls "arguably the greatest of all slave narratives." It comes in the middle of a letter from someone referred to as "Dr. Campbell." After being dazzled by a speech Douglass gave in England in May 1846, Campbell celebrated Douglass for his "mental dimensions," "moral courage," and "all but incomparable _____."

Answer: t _ l _ n _

Nuance Review: "All But" vs. "Almost"

There is some overlap between *all but* and one of the moves—*almost*—that we learned about in chapter 2. Both point to something that is not quite true but is close enough to warrant mention in an effort to signal gradation.

For example, when Jill Leovy writes in *Ghettoside: A True Story of Murder in America* that "in some circles, retaliation for murder was considered <u>all but</u> mandatory," she could have probably written "in some circles, retaliation for murder was considered normal, <u>almost</u> mandatory." And when William Thackeray writes in the classic nineteenth-century novel *Vanity Fair* that one of the characters "felt at that moment an extraordinary, <u>almost</u> irresistible impulse to seize the above-mentioned young woman in his arms, and to kiss her in the face of the company," he could have probably written that the character "felt at that moment an <u>all but</u> irresistible impulse to seize the above-mentioned young woman in his arms, and to kiss her in the face of the company." Rhetorically, these two phrases cover very similar ground.

This is not to say, however, that they're interchangeable. One key difference is that the use of *almost* will often come between two adjectives—"<u>extraordinary</u>, almost <u>irresistible</u>," in the *Vanity Fair* example—while the use of *all but* is usually followed by a single adjective (or verb). Jill Leovy doesn't write "in some circles, retaliation for murder was considered <u>all but</u> mandatory and expected." She writes "in some circles, retaliation for murder was considered <u>all but</u> mandatory."

You'll likely notice additional differences as you see and use both phrases more often. Yet I hope that knowing what they share—and that either could be a good option for certain situations—will open up your writing as well as your thinking to a broader range of expressive opportunities.

TWENTY-TWO

"Where"

There's almost no overlap between the stereotypical personalities of heavy drug users and Parkinson's patients. <u>Where</u> drug users are young and impulsive, Parkinson's patients tend to be elderly and sedate.

—Adam Alter, *Irresistible: The Rise of Addictive Technology and the Business of Keeping Us Hooked* (2017)

<u>Where</u> *[Megan Williams] is pragmatic, Michael Shamberg, the film producer to whom she was long married, is fond of abstractions; <u>where</u> she is always energized, he is somewhat aloof; <u>where</u> she is sparkling and quick, he is meditative and intellectual.*

—Andrew Solomon, *Far from the Tree: Parents, Children, and the Search for Identity* (2012)

Overview

When the word *where* appears at the beginning of a sentence, it usually signals the start of a question. Consider a couple of famous marketing slogans.

- Wendy's (circa 1984): "Where's the beef?"
- Microsoft (circa 1995): "Where do you want to go today?"

Or think about the children's series *Where's Waldo?* and *Where in the World Is Carmen Sandiego?* Each helps reinforce a link instilled in English speakers early in their verbal development: when you use *where*, you'll likely need a question mark as well.

There are exceptions, of course. The titles of two other classic children's books, *Where the Wild Things Are* by Maurice Sendak and *Where the Sidewalk Ends* by Shel Silverstein, are both descriptions—not questions. The same is true of the U2 song "Where the Streets Have No Name." But these outliers do little to disrupt the general pattern. The expectation that *where* functions as an interrogatory remains. It's even built into the "Five W's" of information gathering: *Who? What? Where? When? Why?*

These expectations make it a little more challenging to use *where* in a different way—namely, as the start of a declaratory comparison, like the journalist Kathryn Schulz does in her 2010 book *Being Wrong: Adventures in the Margin of Error*.

> Where the wandering Jew is defined by his sin, the knight errant is distinguished by his virtue; he is explicitly and unfailingly on the side of good.

In these situations, you have to craft your *where* (and the comparison it initiates) so that it's clear that you're not asking a question.

"WHERE"

The business journalist Adam Lashinsky pulls this off in the following excerpt from *Inside Apple: How America's Most Admired—and Secretive—Company Really Works*. He's comparing the management style of Steve Jobs with that of Jobs's successor, Tim Cook. Jobs, Lashinsky says, was somewhat unpredictable (or, in Lashinksy's words, "mercurial"). Cook, in contrast, was steadier and more reserved.

> For his part, Timothy Donald Cook, who is fifty-one, played the trusted aide to Steve Jobs for nearly fifteen years. He was the perfect casting for Apple's long-running buddy movie. <u>Where</u> Jobs was mercurial, Cook was calm.

The cultural historian Tilar Mazzeo creates a similar contrast in *Irena's Children: The Extraordinary Story of the Woman Who Saved 2,500 Children from the Warsaw Ghetto*, her in-depth look at the courageous life of Irena Sandler, the "female Oskar Schindler" who rescued 2,500 children in Nazi-occupied Poland during World War II. Mazzeo compares two sisters Irena befriended, Janka and Jaga.

> Like Irena, Janka was a bit of a free spirit. <u>Where</u> her sister Jaga was straitlaced and sincere, Janka was irreverent and ironic.

Both the example from Lashinsky and the example from Mazzeo put *where* at the beginning of a sentence. But it can also appear in the middle of one. The fiction writer Curtis Sittenfeld takes this approach in *American Wife*, a novel that transports readers into the life and mind of a First Lady of the United States. Here's how she describes two brothers that play key roles in the story.

> [Pete] and Andrew didn't look much alike: They had the same hazel eyes, but Pete didn't have Andrew's impossible eyelashes, and <u>where</u> Andrew was lean and fair, Pete was meaty and had darker hair.

The parallel structure that the *where* creates—"<u>where</u> Andrew was lean and fair, Pete was meaty and had darker hair"—is an additional feature to keep in mind as you make your way through the Notes section and start to think about how to use the move yourself. There's a lyricism to what follows the *where* that can really enhance the power and elegance of a sentence.

Notes

1. **Note how "where" can be used to compare people who have contrasting qualities.**

    "<u>Where</u> my mother was very even-tempered and good-natured, my father was more introspective and a little unapproachable—not meaning to be that way, but just because he was so tired all the time."

    —Alice Waters, *Coming to My Senses: The Making of a Counterculture Cook* (2017)

    "The third was Stanley Edgar Hyman's review of *Tap Roots*, a novel of the South by a white writer. Hyman's style was in dramatic contrast to Ralph [Ellison's]. <u>Where</u> Ralph tended to be self-conscious, solemn, ideological, and ponderous, Hyman was direct, engaging, and smart."

    —Arnold Rampersad, *Ralph Ellison: A Biography* (2007)

2. **Note how "where" can also be used to compare places that have contrasting qualities.**

    "<u>Where</u> South Africa's white countryside was lush and irrigated and green, the black lands were overpopulated and overgrazed, the soil depleted and eroding."

    —Trevor Noah, *Born a Crime* (2016)

    "A bulky barricade ran through the middle of the square, neatly dividing it into two halves. But, <u>where</u> the atmosphere in Chemnitz had been tense, even aggressive, the mood in Landau was largely jubilant. Residents and officials had mounted messages of solidarity with immigrants and refugees on houses around the square."

    —Yascha Mounk, "How a Teen's Death Has Become a Political Weapon" (2019)

3. **Note how "where" doesn't have to come at the beginning of the sentence; it can get tucked in toward the end.**
   "[Bernie] Madoff had sat on the Board of Directors of the Securities Industry Association. No one had heard of Markopolos, who was rumpled <u>where</u> Madoff was smooth, excitable <u>where</u> Madoff was calm."
   —Gary Klein, *Seeing What Others Don't: The Remarkable Ways We Gain Insights* (2013)

4. **Note how "where" can be enhanced by rhetorical repetition.**
   "<u>Where</u> pre-Enlightenment Europe was sporadically cruel, post-Enlightenment Europe was systematically inhumane; <u>where</u> the pre-Enlightenment was haphazardly prejudiced, the Enlightenment was systematically racist, creating a 'scientific' hierarchy of humanity that justified imperialism."
   —Adam Gopnik, "How the Man of Reason Got Radicalized" (2019)

"<u>Where</u> deep practice is a cool, conscious act, ignition is a hot, mysterious burst, an awakening. <u>Where</u> deep practice is an incremental wrapping, ignition works through lightning flashes of image and emotion, evolution-built neural programs that tap into the mind's vast reserves of energy and attention."
   —Daniel Coyle, *The Talent Code* (2009)

5. **Note how a variation of "where" is "whereas."**
   "<u>Whereas</u> Mitchell worked remotely—computing the orbit of Venus from her home in Nantucket and, later, from Vassar—Newcomb worked in the office, then located in Cambridge, Massachusetts."
   —David Baron, *American Eclipse* (2017)

"<u>Whereas</u> we once shared the same temporal rhythms—five days on, two days off, federal holidays, thank-God-it's-Fridays—our weeks are now shaped by the unpredictable dictates of our employers. Nearly a fifth of Americans hold jobs with nonstandard or variable hours."
—Judith Shulevitz, "Why You Never See Your Friends Anymore" (2019)

"When data from one user improves the product for that person, the firm can individually customize it, creating switching costs. When data from one user improves the product for other users, this can—but may not—create network effects. Both kinds of enhancements help provide a barrier to entry, but the former makes existing customers very sticky, <u>whereas</u> the latter provides a key advantage in competing for new customers."
—Andrei Hagiu and Julian Wright, "When Data Creates Competitive Advantage" (2020)

Nuance Practice*

(1) In *Capture: Unraveling the Mystery of Mental Suffering*, David Kessler, who is the former dean of the Yale Medical School, uses the creative yet psychically turbulent lives of several writers, performers, and thinkers to reflect on the various ways the human mind can be taken over and led astray. Among the writers are Virginia Woolf, William James, Robert Lowell, Sylvia Plath, and Tennessee Williams. But the person Kessler focuses on the most is David Foster Wallace, whose decades-long struggle with depression ended in 2008 when he committed suicide at the age of forty-six, in the middle of a career in which he was often revered by many as one of the greatest writers of his generation. In the following passage, Kessler uses *where* twice in a row to highlight the different—and sometimes destructive—lenses through which someone with Foster Wallace's particular blend of psychic torment might interpret the world.

> The same filtering process that helps us avoid an accident is also responsible for selecting which experiences come to define each of our individual realities. <u>Where</u> one person might experience defeat in the face of rejection, another is inspired to act with greater determination. <u>Where</u> David Foster Wallace felt a deep sense of fraudulence and inadequacy, another person might have experienced a profound sense of _____.

(A) aggression
(B) angst
(C) accomplishment
(D) adventure

---

* For answers, see page 210 of the Answer Key.

"WHERE"

(2) In *The General vs. the President*, historian H. W. Brands chronicles the high-stakes political battle between a very popular American general, Douglas A. MacArthur, and a very unpopular (at least at the time) American president, Harry S. Truman. He traces their differences back to their divergent lineages.

> Harry Truman's father had set a different example from MacArthur's. <u>Where</u> military heroes ran in the MacArthur line, marginal farmers and _____ businessmen characterized the Trumans.

(A) successful
(B) entrepreneurial
(C) ambitious
(D) failed

Nuance Review: "Where" and "If"

Chapter 4 introduced a way to use *if* at the beginning of a sentence that shares a lot in common with how we can also use *where*. Both moves produce an elegant, understated form of contrast.

Consider the following *if* sentence from a biography of Thomas Jefferson written in 1918 by the historian David Saville Muzzey, who taught for many years at Columbia University.

> But <u>if</u> Jefferson was an idealist in theory, in practice he was one of the most astute and hard-headed politicians that ever appeared in our public life.

You could pretty easily rewrite that sentence with *where* instead.

> But <u>where</u> Jefferson was an idealist in theory, in practice he was one of the most astute and hard-headed politicians that ever appeared in our public life.

The substitution doesn't always work, however, in the opposite direction. A case in point is a *where* sentence by the journalist Lauren Collins about the interior designs of India Mahdavi.

> <u>Where</u> the L.A. tearoom features birdcage chairs and mirrored daisies, the one in Geneva has an elegant, almost celestial ambience, with tiny starry lights and a fathomless green edging out a darker-than-usual pink as the space's dominant color.

That would be weird as an *if* sentence.

> <u>If</u> the L.A. tearoom features birdcage chairs and mirrored daisies, the one in Geneva has an elegant, almost celestial ambience, with tiny starry lights and a fathomless green edging out a darker-than-usual pink as the space's dominant color.

There is nevertheless some helpful overlap between these two moves. So if you get good at using one, you'll likely also be able to take advantage of the other.

TWENTY-THREE

"But Not"

Whoever wishes to attain an English style, familiar <u>but not</u> coarse, and elegant <u>but not</u> ostentatious, must give his days and nights to the volumes of [Joseph] Addison.

—Samuel Johnson, *Lives of the Poets: Addison, Savage, and Swift* (1779)

Overview

The phrase *but not* helps establish dividing lines. The title of a book on mental health policy in the United States illustrates this effect well. Coauthored by Richard Frank of the Harvard Medical School and Sherry Glied of NYU, it communicates a useful distinction: *Better But Not Well*. "Although there have been substantial improvements in the care and support of mentally ill people," the authors explain, "their situation today is far from ideal." Individuals are doing *better*, but they are by no means doing *well*.

Frank and Glied credit the psychiatrist Gerald Klerman with the clever wording of *Better But Not Well*. Appointed the head of the Alcohol, Drug Abuse, and Mental Health Administration by President Jimmy Carter, Klerman came up with the characterization when surveying the mental health landscape back in 1977.

> Psychiatrists, like their colleagues in internal medicine and neurology, have effective technology that makes the patient better but not well. The patient is better enough to be outside of the institution but not well enough to be fully self-sufficient.

Another notable psychiatrist, Carl Jung, used the same *but not* structure in one of his classic works, *Archetypes and the Collective Unconscious*—or at least the translators of the Princeton University Press version of that book did. Notice the *but not* that appears at the end of the following passage.

> The methodological principle in accordance with which psychology treats the products of the unconscious is this: Contents of an archetypal character are manifestations of processes in the collective unconscious. Hence they do not refer to anything that is or has been conscious, but to something essentially unconscious. In the last analysis, therefore, it is impossible to say what they refer to. Every interpretation necessarily remains

"BUT NOT"

an "as-if." The ultimate core of meaning may be circumscribed, <u>but not</u> described.

Like in the example from Klerman, the *but not* here creates a limit. Jung is saying that we may be able to get a general idea of "the ultimate core of meaning." We may be able to draw a big circle around its dimensions and "circumscribe" it. But we won't be able to identify it completely. We won't be able to "describe" it.

Jung's ideas and language can be tricky to navigate. The examples in the Notes section are far less so. Each gives you a chance to see how *but not* can help clarify claims in a compelling, even snappy way. Each also might remind you of *without being*, which was the move we learned in chapter 20. We'll solidify that connection in the "Nuance Review" that follows the Notes section.

Notes

1. **Note how "but not" helps distinguish between a positive quality and a negative quality.**

    "Over two years passed, and the Schlegel household continued to lead its life of cultured, <u>but not</u> ignoble ease, still swimming gracefully on the grey tides of London."
    —E. M. Forster, *Howards End* (1910)

    "It was four o'clock, breezy, <u>but not</u> windy."
    —Penelope Fitzgerald, "At Hiruharama" in *The Means of Escape* (2000)

    "It was cool <u>but not</u> cold, and Nadia and Saeed stood side by side and did not hold hands but felt the gentle pressure of their arms together, through their sleeves."
    —Mohsin Hamid, *Exit West* (2017)

2. **Note how "but not" often comes in multiples.**

    "She had the eyes of a noticer, cool <u>but not</u> chilly, unsentimental <u>but not</u> hard."
    —Michael Chabon, *Moonglow* (2016)

    "His writing reflects sensitivity to the needs of his reader: it is playful, <u>but not</u> whimsical; descriptive, <u>but not</u> florid; succinct, <u>but not</u> curt."
    —student at the University of Michigan Law School in an assignment for class (2018)

    "He wished to give the impression that he was dotty, <u>but not</u> too dotty. A loony, <u>but not</u> a maniac."
    —Margaret Atwood, *Hag-Seed: William Shakespeare's* The Tempest *Retold* (2016)

3. **Note how "but not" will, on very rare occasions, follow a semicolon, breaking with more conventional uses of that punctuation mark.**

"The psychiatrist said, 'Wait a minute.' His voice was friendly, concerned; <u>but not</u> patronizing."

—Charles Beaumont, *Perchance to Dream* (1958)

NOTES ON NUANCE

Nuance Practice*

(1) In 2003, the science journalist Mary Roach earned a spot on the *New York Times* best sellers list with a book called *Stiff: The Curious Lives of Human Cadavers*. Among the more interesting chapters is one that introduces Dennis Shanahan, an injury analyst hired to investigate the dead bodies on TWA Flight 800, which exploded on its way from New York to Paris in July 1996. Fill in the word that comes after *but not* in the following description.

> For Shanahan, the hardest thing about Flight 800 was that most of the bodies were relatively whole. "Intactness bothers me much more than the lack of it," he says. The sorts of things most of us can't imagine seeing or coping with—severed hands, legs, scraps of flesh—Shanahan is more comfortable with. "That way, it's just tissue. You can put yourself in that frame of mind and get on with your job. It's gory, <u>but not</u> ____. Gore you get used to. Shattered lives you don't."

(A) serious
(B) sad
(C) secretive
(D) satirical

(2) One of the humorist David Sedaris's big breaks came when he read his story "Santaland Diaries" on NPR in 1992. The story focuses on his time working as a Christmas elf at a Macy's department store in New York. He later published it in the essay collection *Barrel Fever*. See if you can figure out the missing word in the following excerpt.

---

* For answers, see page 210 of the Answer Key.

"BUT NOT"

I spend all day lying to people, saying "You look so pretty," and "Santa can't wait to visit with you. You're all he talks about. It's just not Christmas without you. You're Santa's favorite person in the entire tri-state area." Sometimes I lay it on real thick: "Aren't you the Princess of Rongovia? Santa said a beautiful Princess was here to visit him. He said she would be wearing a red dress and that she was very pretty, but not stuck up or _____. That's you, isn't it?" I lay it on and the parents mouth the words "Thank you" and "Good job."

(A) two-faced
(B) beautiful
(C) kind
(D) outgoing

NOTES ON NUANCE

Nuance Review: "But Not" and "Without Being"

(1) The effect of *but not* is very similar to the effect of *without being*, which was a move we looked at back in chapter 20. Compare these two versions of an excerpt from "The Lees of Happiness," a short story F. Scott Fitzgerald published in 1922, right in the middle of the Jazz Age.

> A. During dinner the twilight faltered into dusk, and later it was a starry dark outside, filled and permeated with the frail gorgeousness of Roxanne's white dress and her tremulous, low laugh.
>
> Such a little girl she is, thought Harry. Not as old as Kitty.
>
> He compared the two. Kitty—nervous <u>without being</u> sensitive, temperamental without temperament, a woman who seemed to flit and never light—and Roxanne, who was as young as spring night, and summed up in her own adolescent laughter.
>
> B. During dinner the twilight faltered into dusk, and later it was a starry dark outside, filled and permeated with the frail gorgeousness of Roxanne's white dress and her tremulous, low laugh.
>
> Such a little girl she is, thought Harry. Not as old as Kitty.
>
> He compared the two. Kitty—nervous <u>but not</u> sensitive, temperamental without temperament, a woman who seemed to flit and never light—and Roxanne, who was as young as spring night, and summed up in her own adolescent laughter.

Fitzgerald went with option A (*without being*), but both options seem capable of conveying the same point.

(2) A similar substitution could be imagined in the following blurb for *Commentary* magazine, a publication that has been engaging in high-level discourse about politics and culture since launching its first issue in 1945:

> Every month in print, and every day online, *Commentary* somehow manages to pull off a dazzling balancing act: intellectual but unpretentious, serious but never boring, timely <u>but not</u> fleeting.

The blurb comes from Yuval Levin, who edits another respected magazine, *National Affairs*. He could have easily framed it with *without being* instead.

> Every month in print, and every day online, *Commentary* somehow manages to pull off a dazzling balancing act: intellectual but unpretentious, serious but never boring, timely <u>without being</u> fleeting.

TWENTY-FOUR

Nuance Spotlight

THE ECONOMIST

That there is value in quality journalism is hardly surprising to those who drive media content. That there can be so much value in consistency of voice is far less appreciated. The Economist's readers aren't just looking for smarts or individuality—they can get that from many sources. They're looking for someone to help them make sense of events, with a coherent and consistent point of view.

—Bharat Anand, *The Content Trap: A Strategist's Guide to Digital Change* (2016)

Overview

I remember hearing a helpful bit of advice when I was in law school, although I imagine it could apply to folks pursuing other professions as well: "Write like . . . *The Economist*."

The person didn't mean that I should necessarily adopt *The Economist*'s politics or its practice of leaving articles unsigned. But they did want me to embrace its crisp, informative style. Place a premium on precision, the person insisted. Value logic, facts, and readability. Don't get seduced by jargon.

I have since discovered another benefit. If you try to write like *The Economist*, you get to practice many of the nuance moves we've been learning in this book, given how often those come up in the publication's pages and online posts. I've included only a small selection in this sample. If you check out an issue or two yourself, you'll likely find several more. There is an admirable elegance to *The Economist*'s well-crafted efficiency.

* * *

For more information about *The Economist*, visit their "About Us" page at https://www.economist.com/help/about-us. Here are some key excerpts.

On why its articles are anonymous: "Many hands write *The Economist*, but it speaks with a collective voice. Leaders are discussed, often disputed, each week in meetings that are open to all members of the editorial staff. Journalists often co-operate on articles. And some articles are heavily edited. The main reason for anonymity, however, is a belief that what is written is more important than who writes it. As Geoffrey Crowther, editor from 1938 to 1956, put it, anonymity keeps the editor 'not the master but the servant of something far greater than himself. You can call that ancestor-worship if you wish, but it gives to the paper an astonishing momentum of thought and principle.'"

On why it's written the way it is: "*The Economist* believes in plain language. Walter Bagehot, our most famous 19th-century editor, tried 'to be conversational, to put things in the most direct and picturesque manner, as people would talk to each other in common speech, to remember and use expressive colloquialisms.' That remains the style of the paper today."

Notes

1. To

"American influence on global (not just British) English is rising. But varieties from Ireland <u>to</u> India <u>to</u> Australia retain a clear identity."

—"Fears of British English's Disappearance Are Overblown," *The Economist* (2017)

2. What _ Is To _

"Glencore is to mining <u>what</u> Goldman Sachs <u>is to</u> high-street banking: nominally in the same trade but in a turbo-charged way."

—"Glencore's Attempt at Reinventing Mining Has Run into Trouble," *The Economist* (2018)

3. All But

"A week after a general election rocked by suspicions of fraud, the dust is beginning to settle. It looks <u>all but</u> certain that Imran Khan, a former captain of Pakistan's cricket team, will be sworn in as the country's next prime minister."

—"How Will Imran Khan Govern?" (2018)

4. At Once

"In many ways, the 39-year-old Mr. Macron is not yet well understood. Behind the haughty exterior, a leader is emerging who seems to be <u>at once</u> brave, disciplined and thoughtful."

—"The Spotlight Shifts from Germany to France" (2017)

5. If

"The prime minister's own backbenchers are feverishly (<u>if</u> ineptly) plotting to bring her down."

—"The Truth about a No-Deal Brexit" (2018)

NUANCE SPOTLIGHT

6. Albeit

"At the moment Katla, one of Iceland's largest volcanoes, located near the island's southern tip, sleeps beneath 700 meters of ice. It has so slept, <u>albeit</u> fitfully, for almost 100 years."

—"Events in Iceland Explain Years of Famine in Europe's Dark Ages" (2017)

7. As

"Consider the experience of a multinational carmaker, <u>as</u> revealing <u>as</u> it is commonplace."

—"After the Deluge: Business and the Effects of Global Warming" (2019)

8. Chiasmus

"When it is a <u>matter</u> of <u>opinion</u>, make your <u>opinion matter</u>."

—advertising slogan (2019)

TWENTY-FIVE

Double Moves

Why would any species—<u>let alone</u> many separate species—evolve an entirely new way to sing when the traditional avian vocal songs had been working fine, <u>even</u> gloriously, for over seventy million years?

—Richard Prum, The Evolution of Beauty (2017)

This tableau is oddly reminiscent of the search for extraterrestrial intelligence: the signals piped out over the border, from one domain to another <u>as</u> alien <u>as</u> it is infinite, with such poignant hopefulness that may be heard at all, <u>much less</u> understood.

—Caitrin Keiper, "Do Elephants Have Souls?" (2013)

Overview

We've now come to the twenty-fifth and final chapter. So it seems fitting to highlight a nice consequence of making it through the previous twenty-four: the more moves you learn, the more likely you are to notice when two different ones show up in the same sentence.

Perhaps you've had that experience already. When reading chapter 3, for instance, one of the examples we used to understand the "A-B-B-A" move known as chiasmus also included the *un-* move from chapter 1.

> In Paris we have a <u>beautiful existence</u> but not a <u>full life</u>, and in New York we have a <u>full life</u> but an <u>unbeautiful existence</u>.
> —Adam Gopnik, *Paris to the Moon* (2000)

Or maybe you caught the double move in chapter 22. That's the chapter that taught us how to use *where* to set up a stylish comparison. One of the model sentences contains another move as well: *even* from chapter 2.

> A bulky barricade ran through the middle of the square, neatly dividing it into two halves. But, <u>where</u> the atmosphere in Chemnitz had been tense, <u>even</u> aggressive, the mood in Landau was largely jubilant. Residents and officials had mounted messages of solidarity with immigrants and refugees on houses around the square.
> —Yascha Mounk, "How a Teen's Death Has Become a Political Weapon" (2019)

You'll find additional combinations below. Each is from a source we haven't looked at yet.

1. **Where + Almost**
    "<u>Where</u> Adams was stout, Jefferson was lean and long-limbed, <u>almost</u> bony."
    —David McCullough, *John Adams* (2001)

2. **However + At Once**
    "Simon, walking in front of Ralph, felt a flicker of incredulity—a beast with claws that scratched, that sat on a mountaintop, that left no tracks and yet was not fast enough to catch Samneric. <u>However</u> Simon thought of the beast, there rose before his inward sight the picture of a human <u>at once</u> heroic and sick."
    —William Golding, *Lord of the Flies* (1954)

3. **Less Than + All But**
    "On the third day, all sides found a way to come together. Stalin made a <u>less than</u> subtle suggestion that failure to open a second front in Europe in 1944 could <u>all but</u> ensure that a war-weary Soviet Union would seek a separate peace with Hitler."
    —Jay Winik, *1944: FDR and the Year That Changed History* (2015)

4. **As + Chiasmus**
    "We were <u>as happy as</u> we were <u>poor</u>, or <u>as poor as</u> we were <u>happy</u>—phrase it to suit yourself."
    —Mark Twain, "Is He Living or Is He Dead?" (1893)

It's possible you'll someday come across a sentence with three or more nuance moves in it. But I caution you against packing your own writing with too many moves. As I stressed way back in the introduction, a key part of nuance is restraint. Showy writing is rarely effective writing.

Yet what I hope this book has helped you see is that there are ways to expand and enhance your menu of rhetorical options. Across a wide variety of fields, styles, and mediums, we can all learn to do a good deal more with our written words than we might have previously imagined.

ANSWER KEY

Chapter 1: "Un-"
Nuance Practice

(1) Answer: (B) ungimmicky
(2) Answer: (B) unpuzzled
(3) Answer: (C) Virginia Woolf
(4) Answer: (D) un-Manhattan
(5) Answer: *King Lear*

Chapter 2: "Almost" and "Even"
Nuance Practice

(1) Answer: (B) humble
(2) Answer: (D) bucolic
(3) Answer: Rome
(4) Answer: Leo Tolstoy

Chapter 3: Chiasmus ("A-B-B-A")

Nuance Practice

(1)

Slogan	Company
"Love the Taste. Taste the Love."	Jimmy John's
"The King of Hotels and the Hotel of Kings"	Ritz-Carlton
"It's Not How Fast You Mow; It's How You Mow Fast."	John Deere
"No Change Fees: Because Sometimes 9–5 Becomes 5–9"	Southwest Airlines

(2) Answer: (D) Bacon
(3) Answer: (C) Sinclair Lewis
(4) Answer: "It is fundamentally the confusion between effectiveness and efficiency that stands between doing the right things and doing *things right*." (emphasis added)

Chapter 4: "If"—"If"—"If Not"

Nuance Practice

(1) Answer: (B) Bernie Madoff
(2) Answer: (C) the map

Nuance Review

(1) Answer: (B) almost
(2) Answer: (C) even

ANSWER KEY

Chapter 5: "As"

Nuance Practice

(1) Answer: Oscar Wilde
(2) Answer: (D) *Invisible Man*

Nuance Practice: Henry Kissinger

(1) Answer: (C) unconvincing
(2) Answer: (A) unwise
(3) Answer: (D) tortuous

Chapter 6: Nuance Spotlight (Jane Austen)

There are no answers for this chapter because there was no "Nuance Practice" section.

Chapter 7: "At Once"

Nuance Practice

(1) Answer: (B) augmented
(2) Answer: maintaining
(3) Answer: Harry Truman
(4) Answer: The name of the novel is *The Kite **Runner***.

Chapter 8: "Equal Parts"

Nuance Practice

(1) Answer: (B) old South
(2) Answer: (B) worry

Nuance Review

(1) Answer: (A) equal parts
(2) Answer: (B) at once
(3) Answer: (B) at once

ANSWER KEY

Chapter 9: "To"

Nuance Practice

Quote	*Source*
"Today Apache is one of the most successful open-source tools, powering about two thirds of the web sites in the world. And because Apache can be downloaded for free anywhere in the world, people from Russia to South Africa to Vietnam use it to create web sites."	Thomas Friedman, *The World Is Flat* (2005)
"Several generations of start-ups have tapped these dynamics to build dominant positions, from eBay to Facebook to Airbnb. To accomplish these goals, it's crucial to develop a rigorous understanding of how network effects work."	Chris Yeh and Reid Hoffman, *Blitzscaling: The Lightning-Fast Path to Building Massively Valuable Companies* (2018)
"His writing, moreover, had already been hailed as 'exceedingly brilliant,' and praised by everyone from the Prime Minister to Arthur Conan Doyle."	Candice Millard, *Hero of the Empire: The Boer War, a Daring Escape, and the Making of Winston Churchill* (2016)

(2) Answer: (B) Nairobi

ANSWER KEY

Chapter 10: "Albeit"

Nuance Practice

(1) Answer: (C) briefly
(2) Answer: (C) decade
(3) See the chart below for answers

Quote	Source
"Today, there are some 115 index mutual funds designed to track the S&P 500 Index. Astonishingly, more than half of them carry an initial sales load, albeit often concealed by offering class 'B' shares with no front-end load but with an additional heavy annual fee (used to pay the broker)."	John Bogle, *The Little Book of Common Sense Investing* (2007)
"While we can never know what would have happened if the Court had not acted as it did (if *Brown* had never been decided or had come out the other way), the existence and strength of the pro-civil-rights forces at least suggest that change would have occurred, albeit at a pace unknown."	Gerald N. Rosenberg, *The Hollow Hope: Can Courts Bring About Social Change?* (1991)
"We must not accept the state of corruption as if it were just another sin: even though corruption is often identified with sin, in fact they are two distinct realities, albeit interconnected."	Pope Francis, *The Name of God Is Mercy* (2016)

ANSWER KEY

Chapter 11: "However"

Nuance Practice: Confessions

(1) Answer: (A) hungry
(2) Answer: (C) just
(3) Answer: (B) ignorant

Nuance Practice: World War II

(1) Answer: (C) *Korematsu v. United States*
(2) Answer: (D) insincerely
(3) Answer: Winston Churchill

Chapter 12: "At Best, At Worst"

Nuance Practice

(1) Answer: (C) locked
(2) Answer: (A) unruly
(3) Answer: Amy Poehler

Chapter 13: Nuance Spotlight (James Baldwin)

There are no answers for this chapter because there was no "Nuance Practice" section.

Chapter 14: "What __ Is to __"

Nuance Practice

(1) Answer: (B) Vatican
(2) Answer: (C) Henry Ford
(3) Answer: (D) Thomas Edison

ANSWER KEY

Chapter 15: "Let Alone" and "Much Less"
Nuance Practice

Quote	Source
"'Care of land depends on people who are not in a constant emergency, who know it well and who will take care of it well,' Mary says. 'So, to have that, we've got to have an economy that makes it possible for those people to even exist, much less survive.'"	*The Bitter Southerner*: Jodi Cash, "Leveling the Field for Family Farms" (2017)
"She and Dolly took turns filling me in. I'd never heard of the Funny River, much less the fire that had ravaged the Kenai. They told me a body had been found, and that its DNA had been tested."	*The Atlantic*: Alex Tizon, "In the Land of Missing Persons" (2016)
"Tony is 51, has high cholesterol, and recently had malignant carcinomas excised from his back and ankle. 'I need my kids prepared for life after Dad,' he says. Peyton couldn't hit a nail with a hammer, let alone brush his teeth or buy groceries. So in the fall of 2014, Tony enrolled him at the E. H. Gentry Facility in Talladega, Alabama, a rehabilitation program for adults with sensory disabilities that focuses on independent living."	*Esquire*: Jessica Pishko, "The FBI Accused Him of Terrorism. He Couldn't Tie His Shoes" (2016)
"Courts only assess guilt or innocence before a conviction. After that, appellate courts focus solely on fairness. Did everyone follow the rules and live up to their duties? Getting a re-hearing of the facts is a monumental, often decades-long quest through a legal thicket. Most defendants never get to start the process, let alone win."	*The Atlantic*: Megan Rose and ProPublica, "The Deal Prosecutors Offer When They Have No Cards Left to Play" (2017)
"It is hard to design a memorial, let alone a Holocaust museum."	*Commentary*: Ben Schachter, "Forgetful Architecture" (2010)

ANSWER KEY

Chapter 16: "As Diverse As"

Nuance Practice

(1) Answer: Moldova

(2) Answer: Bruce Springsteen

Chapter 17: "More ___ Than ___"

Nuance Practice

(1) Answer: (B) pleased, (A) physics

(2) Answer: (B) Norman Rockwell

(3) Answer: (A) Abercrombie

Chapter 18: "Less ___ Than ___" and "Less Than"

Nuance Practice: "Less ___ Than ___"

(1) Answer: (D) Rooseveltian

(2) Answer: security

Nuance Practice: "Less Than ___"

Phrase	Word Bank Match
"The room was as it had been before: only a bed with a bare mattress that was <u>less than</u> _____."	clean
"Yet the woman seemed to find his answer <u>less than</u> _____."	satisfying
"They were oblivious to the gasps and slammed brakes that accompanied their sudden and daring lane changes, and to the <u>less-than-</u>_____ words directed at them by their fellow drivers."	complimentary
"Thus when Oba, who ran the garage where he serviced his car, recommended a young woman to be his personal driver, Kafuku looked <u>less than</u> _____."	thrilled

ANSWER KEY

Chapter 19: Nuance Spotlight (William F. Buckley Jr.)

There are no answers for this chapter because there was no "Nuance Practice" section.

Chapter 20: "Without Being" and "Without"
Nuance Practice

(1) Answer: (B) muscular
(2) Answer: (C) quiet
(3) Answer: (C) convincing

Chapter 21: "All But"
Nuance Practice

(1)

Phrase	Word Bank Match
"Douglass was and is a hero; he has been <u>all but</u> _____ as a national figure in Ireland, Scotland, and Britain. His *Narrative* is read all over the world."	adopted
"A delegation of friends gathered at the docks to meet him. But so anxious was Douglass to see his family, he <u>all but</u> _____ to the train that took him to Lynn within a half hour."	ran
"Perhaps the thing in life he needed most was <u>all but</u> _____ beyond his grasp, and certainly not achievable in one woman. Douglass might cling to some of the female relationships in his life at the same time any profoundly deep love may have been an unbearable intensity."	forever

(2) Answer: talent

ANSWER KEY

Chapter 22: "Where"
Nuance Practice

(1) Answer: (C) accomplishment
(2) Answer: (D) failed

Chapter 23: "But Not"
Nuance Practice

(1) Answer: (B)
(2) Answer: (A)

Chapter 24: Nuance Spotlight (*The Economist*)

There are no answers for this chapter because there was no "Nuance Practice" section.

Chapter 25: Double Moves

There are no answers for this chapter because there was no "Nuance Practice" section.

PHOTO CREDITS

One

Look Magazine. "Ernest Hemingway Writing at Campsite in Kenya." *National Archives*. https://catalog.archives.gov/id/192655. Courtesy of the National Archives and Records Administration, which has put this image in the public domain.

George Charles Beresford. "Portrait of Virginia Woolf." *Wikimedia Commons*. Last edited July 26, 2016. https://commons.wikimedia.org/wiki/File:George _Charles_Beresford_-_Virginia_Woolf_in_1902_-_Restoration.jpg. This image is in the public domain.

Two

Arnold Newman. "Photo Portrait of President Lyndon B. Johnson in the Oval Office." *Wikimedia Commons*. Last edited November 29, 2017. https://en.wikipedia.org/wiki/File:37_Lyndon_Johnson_3x4.jpg. Courtesy of White House Press Office.

Marion Trikosko. "Martin Luther King Leaning on a Lectern." *Wikimedia Commons*. Last edited August 5, 2006. https://commonswikimedia.org/wiki/File:Martin-Luther-King-1964-leaning-on-a-lectern.jpg. Courtesy of U.S. News & World Report Magazine Photograph Collection at the Library of Congress.

Joshua Reynolds. "Edward Gibbon." *Wikimedia Commons*. Last edited November 14, 2012. https://commons.wikimedia.org/wiki/File:Edward_Emily _Gibbon.jpg. This image is in the public domain.

PHOTO CREDITS

Ilya Repin. "Portrait of Lev Nikolayevich Tolstoy." *Wikimedia Commons*. Last edited March 26, 2018. https://commons.wikimedia.org/wiki/File:Ilya_Efimovich_Repin_(1844-1930)_-_Portrait_of_Leo_Tolstoy_(1887).jpg. This image is in the public domain.

Three

"Francis Bacon" by RaphaelMoreno0601 is available under CC BY-SA 4.0.

"Drucker" by Jeff McNeill is available under CC BY-SA 2.0.

Five

Napoleon Sarony. "Oscar Wilde." *Wikimedia Commons*. Last edited December 5, 2008. https://commons.wikimedia.org/wiki/File:Oscar_Wilde_portrait.jpg. This image is in the public domain.

"Ralph Ellison photo portrait seated" by the United States Information Agency is available in the public domain.

"Henry Kissinger" by Marion S. Trikosko is available in the public domain.

Six

"Jane Austen coloured version" by an unknown author is available in the public domain.

Seven

"Portrait of President Harry S. Truman." *Wikimedia Commons*. Last edited January 28, 2018. https://commons.wikimedia.org/wiki/File:TRUMAN_58-766-06.jpg. Courtesy of the National Archives and Records Administration, which has put this in the public domain.

Eleven

"Sir Winston Churchill." *Wikimedia Commons*. Last edited October 28, 2010. https://commons.wikimedia.org/wiki/File:Sir_Winston_S_Churchill.jpg. This image was produced by the US Federal Government and is in the public domain.

PHOTO CREDITS

Thirteen

Carl Van Vechten. "James Baldwin." *Wikimedia Commons*. Last edited December 2, 2009. https://commons.wikimedia.org/wiki/File:Jamesbaldwin.jpg. This image is in the public domain and can be found in the Van Vechten Collection at the Library of Congress.

Fourteen

Edward S. Curtis. "The North American Indian." *Wikimedia Commons*. Last edited December 10, 2013. https://commons.wikimedia.org/wiki/File:Edward_S._Curtis_Geronimo_Apache_cp01002v.jpg. The portrait is of Geronimo, the famous Apache. The image is in the public domain.

"Portrait of Henry Ford." *Wikimedia Commons*. Last edited August 3, 2014. https://commons.wikimedia.org/wiki/File:Henry_ford_1919.jpg. Courtesy of the United States Library of Congress's Prints and Photographs division. This image is in the public domain.

"Thomas Edison." *Wikimedia Commons*. Last edited May 6, 2010. https://commons.wikimedia.org/wiki/File:Thomas_edison_glühbirne.jpg. Courtesy of the National Archives and Records Administration. This image is in the public domain.

Sixteen

Pete Souza. "Bruce Springsteen Receiving the Presidential Medal of Freedom." *Wikimedia Commons*. Last edited August 12, 2006. https://commons.wikimedia.org/wiki/File:Bruce_Springsteen_Presidential_Medal_of_Freedom.jpg. This image is in the public domain.

Eighteen

Harris & Ewing. "George F. Kennan." *Library of Congress*. *Wikimedia Commons*. Last edited March 12, 2018. https://www.loc.gov/pictures/collection/hec/item/2016870504/. Courtesy of the Harris & Ewing Collection at the Library of Congress.

PHOTO CREDITS

Nineteen

Bert Goulait. "William F. Buckley, Jr. Attends the Second Inauguration of President Ronald Reagan." *Wikimedia Commons*. Last edited March 12, 2018. https://commons.wikimedia.org/wiki/File:William_F._Buckley,_Jr._1985.jpg. This image is in the public domain.

Twenty-one

George K. Warren. "Frederick Douglass." *Wikimedia Commons*. Last edited August 12, 2006. https://commons.wikimedia.org/wiki/File:Frederick_Douglass_(circa_1879).jpg. Courtesy of the National Archives and Records Administration, which has put this in the public domain.

NOTES

Introduction

4 Elizabeth L. Bjork & Robert Bjork, Making Things Hard on Yourself, but in a Good Way: Creating Desirable Difficulties to Enhance Learning, https://bjorklab.psych.ucla.edu/wp-content/uploads/sites/13/2016/04/EBjork_RBjork_2011.pdf; Peter C. Brown et al., Make It Stick: The Science of Successful Learning 67–101 (2014).

One

7 Colum McCann, TransAtlantic 284–85 (2013).
7 Karan Mahajan, The Association of Small Bombs 68 (2016).
8 *See* The Best American Short Stories of the Century 720–34 (John Updike & Katrina Kenison eds., 2010).
8 Gish Jen, *Birthmates*, 20 Ploughshares 81, 95 (1994).
8 Ta-Nehisi Coates, *The Black Family in the Age of Mass Incarceration*, Atlantic (Oct. 2015), https://www.theatlantic.com/magazine/archive/2015/10/the-black-family-in-the-age-of-mass-incarceration/403246/.
9 *Regina v. Dudley & Stephens*, 14 Q.B.D. 273, 286–87 (1884).
9 George Eliot, Middlemarch 645 (Digireads.com 2016) (1871).
9 Amy McDonald, *Uncola: Seven-Up, Counterculture and the Making of an American Brand*, The Devil's Tale (Dec. 4, 2017), https://blogs.library.duke.edu/rubenstein/2017/12/04/uncola/.

NOTES

9 *The Un-carrier Goes "All In": T-Mobile ONE Now Includes Taxes & Fees*, T-MOBILE (Jan. 4, 2017), https://www.t-mobile.com/news/un-carrier-next.

9 *Make It an Unwich*, JIMMY JOHN'S GOURMET SANDWICHES, https://www.jimmyjohns.com/unwich-info/ (last visited Apr. 10, 2019); Anna B., *High Protein Options at Jimmy John's*, DELISHABLY (Jan. 12, 2017), https://delishably.com/dining-out/High-Protein-Options-at-Jimmy-Johns.

9 Resource/Ammirati, an IBM Company, *Labatt: Get Undomesticated (Wakeboard)*, YOUTUBE (Nov. 24, 2015), https://www.youtube.com/watch?v=KUndBAHtuU4.

9 Tessa Hadley, *Cecilia Awakened*, NEW YORKER (Sept. 17, 2018), https://www.newyorker.com/magazine/2018/09/17/cecilia-awakened.

10 HOPE JAHREN, LAB GIRL 132 (2016).

10 Chinua Achebe, *The Voter, in* GIRLS AT WAR 13 (Anchor 1991).

10 George Orwell, *Politics and the English Language, in* THE COLLECTED ESSAYS, JOURNALISM AND LETTERS OF GEORGE ORWELL 138n1 (Sonia Orwell & Ian Angus eds., 1968).

11 WILLIAM FINNEGAN, BARBARIAN DAYS: A SURFING LIFE 5 (2016).

11 Austin Murphy, Barbarian Days: *William Finnegan's Surfing Memoir Is a Glorious Ride*, SPORTS ILLUSTRATED (July 22, 2015), https://www.si.com/edge/2015/07/22/barbarian-days-william-finnegan-surfing-memoir-book-review.

11 Ernest Hemingway, *The Capital of the World, in* THE COMPLETE SHORT STORIES OF ERNEST HEMINGWAY 29 (Finca Vigía ed., Simon & Schuster 1998).

12 Emily Temple, *Famous Last Words: 15 Authors' Epitaphs*, FLAVORWIRE (Oct. 22, 2012), http://flavorwire.com/339429/famous-last-words-15-authors-epitaphs/.

12 David Gilbert, *The Sightseers*, NEW YORKER (Nov. 20, 2017), https://www.newyorker.com/magazine/2017/11/20/the-sightseers.

13 JAMES SHAPIRO, THE YEAR OF LEAR 52 (2006).

Two

15 DONNA TARTT, THE SECRET HISTORY 34 (1992).

15 DAVID MICHAELIS, SCHULZ AND PEANUTS: A BIOGRAPHY 396 (2007).

16 VLADIMIR VLADIMIROVICH NABOKOV, LOLITA 293 (1997).

16 Louise Erdrich, The Round House 15 (2005).
17 Jeff Hobbs, The Short and Tragic Life of Robert Peace 167 (2014).
17 Karl Ove Knausgaard, My Struggle (Book 2): A Man in Love 24 (Don Bartlett trans., 2014).
17 Jonathan Franzen, *Introduction* to The Best American Essays xv (Jonathan Franzen ed., Robert Atwan series ed., 2016).
18 Edwidge Danticat, *Seven*, N.Y. Times (Oct. 1, 2001), https://www.newyorker.com/magazine/2001/10/01/seven; The Best American series, The Best American Short Stories 38 (Sue Miller ed., Katrina Kenison series ed., 2002).
18 Grant Gilmore, The Ages of American Law 67 (2d ed. 2014).
18 Siddhartha Mukherjee, The Gene: An Intimate History 4 (2016).
18 Octavia E. Butler, Fledgling 198 (2005).
18 Patricia Highsmith, The Price of Salt, or Carol 34 (1952).
19 Mary Oliver, A Poetry Handbook 24 (1994).
19 *INS v. Chadha*, 462 U.S. 919, 959 (1983).
19 Charles Dickens, A Tale of Two Cities 45 (Wordsworth Editions 1993).
19 Michael Lewis, The Undoing Project: A Friendship That Changed Our Minds (2016).
20 Tom Perrotta, The Abstinence Teacher 353 (2007).
20 M. F. K. Fisher, *M. F. K. Fisher on the Basics*, Lapham's Q. (1949), https://www.laphamsquarterly.org/food/mfk-fisher-basics.
20 Dan Howell, *Chicago Epithalamion*, Poetry Found. (Jan. 2004), https://www.poetryfoundation.org/poetrymagazine/browse?volume=183&issue=4&page=16.
20 Stephen Dunn, *Dismantling the House*, Poetry Found. (Feb. 2003), https://www.poetryfoundation.org/poetrymagazine/browse?contentId=41749.
21 Robert Caro, Master of the Senate: The Years of Lyndon Johnson III (2002) (book blurb from Patrick Beach, *Austin-American Statesman*).
21 Robert Caro, Means of Ascent: The Years of Lyndon Johnson II (1991) (book blurb from Robert Massie).
21 Michael Schaub, *"Power": Robert Caro's Life of Johnson Hits the '60s*, NPR (May 2, 2012), https://www.npr.org/2012/05/02/151459406/power-robert-caros-life-of-johnson-hits-the-60s.

NOTES

21 Robert A. Caro, Master of the Senate: The Years of Lyndon Johnson III 340 (2002).
22 Hampton Sides, Hellhound on His Trail: The Stalking of Martin Luther King Jr. and the International Hunt for His Assassin 4 (2010).
23 Edward Gibbon, The Decline and Fall of the Roman Empire: Volume III 545 (abr. ed., Modern Library 2003) (1776).
23 Leo Tolstoy, Resurrection 379 (Louise Maude trans., Dover Giant Thrift ed. 2016) (1899).

Three

25 Larry McMurtry, Lonesome Dove 44 (1985).
25 Yaa Gyasi, Homegoing 28 (2016).
26 Christopher McDougall, Born to Run 202, 204 (2009).
26 Eric Brandt, *Harley-Davidson's New Campaign Spotlights Freedom by Motorcycle*, The Drive (Aug. 17, 2017), https://www.thedrive.com/watch-this/13581/harley-davidsons-new-campaign-spotlights-freedom-by-motorcycle.
26 Alexandre Dumas, The Three Musketeers 95 (Eleanor Hochman trans., Signet Classics 2006) (1844).
26 Ward Farnsworth, Farnsworth's Classical English Rhetoric 98 (2010).
26 *Id.* at 108.
27 *Id.* at 98.
28 Andrew Solomon, The Noonday Demon: An Atlas of Depression 16 (2001).
28 *Brown v. Allen*, 344 U.S. 443, 540 (1953) (Jackson, J., concurring).
28 Herodotus, Herodotus: The Histories (Penguin Classics 1996) (circa 440 BCE).
28 Frederick Douglass, Narrative of the Life of Frederick Douglass, an American Slave (Dover 1995) (1849).
28 *Marbury v. Madison*, 5 U.S. 137, 178 (1803).
29 Adam Gopnik, Paris to the Moon 336 (2000).
29 Louis Menand, *The De Man Case*, New Yorker (Mar. 24, 2014), https://www.newyorker.com/magazine/2014/03/24/the-de-man-case.
29 Nate Silver, The Signal and the Noise: Why So Many Predictions Fail—but Some Don't 39 (2012).

29   Kara Swisher, *The Money Shot*, Vanity Fair (June 2013), https://www.vanityfair.com/news/business/2013/06/kara-swisher-instagram.

29   Greyston Bakery, Company Website, https://greystonbakery.com/pages/about-greyston (last visited Feb. 17, 2019).

29   President John F. Kennedy, Inaugural Address in Washington, DC (Jan. 20, 1961).

30   Dr. Seuss, Horton Hatches the Egg (1940).

30   Rudyard Kipling, The Second Jungle Book 29 (1895).

30   A. A. Milne, Winnie the Pooh and the Blustery Day (1968).

31   Francis Bacon, *The Advancement of Learning*, in The Advance of Learning Book I with Notes by F. G. Selby 38 (1898).

32   Sinclair Lewis, It Can't Happen Here 18 (1935).

32   Peter F. Drucker, *Managing for Business Effectiveness*, Harv. Bus. Rev. (May 1963), https://hbr.org/1963/05/managing-for-business-effectiveness.

Four

33   Yuval Noah Harari, Sapiens: A Brief History of Humankind 94 (2011).

33   Maya Angelou, Hallelujah! The Welcome Table: A Lifetime of Memories with Recipes 85 (2004).

33   Charles Fishman and Brian Grazer, A Curious Mind: The Secret to a Bigger Life 14 (2015).

34   Carlo Rovelli, Seven Brief Lessons on Physics 23 (2016).

34   Lucy Grealy, Autobiography of a Face 112 (2016).

34   John Lanchester, *When Bitcoin Grows Up*, 38 London Review of Books 3, 3–12 (2016), https://www.lrb.co.uk/v38/n08/john-lanchester/when-bitcoin-grows-up.

35   Paule Marshall, *From the Poets in the Kitchen*, N.Y. Times (Jan. 9, 1983), https://www.nytimes.com/1983/01/09/books/from-the-poets-in-the-kitchen.html.

35   Christopher Beach, The Cambridge Introduction to American Poetry 13 (2003).

35   Hannah Arendt, Eichmann in Jerusalem: A Report on the Banality of Evil 11 (Penguin Classics 2006).

35   George Orwell, The Collected Essays, Journalism and Letters of George Orwell 137 (Sonia Orwell & Ian Angus eds.,

vol. 4, 1946), https://faculty.washington.edu/rsoder/EDLPS579/HonorsOrwellPoliticsEnglishLanguage.pdf.

36 ROBERT SCHILLER, NARRATIVE ECONOMICS: HOW STORIES GO VIRAL AND DRIVE MAJOR ECONOMIC EVENTS 148 (2019).

36 JOHN GUY, QUEEN OF SCOTS: THE TRUE LIFE OF MARY STUART 139–40 (2004).

36 Ghaith Abdul-Ahad, *The Baghdad Road*, 39 LONDON REVIEW OF BOOKS 32 (2017), https://www.lrb.co.uk/v39/n09/ghaith-abdul-ahad/the-baghdad-road.

36 Ernest Hemingway, *The Capital of the World*, *in* THE COMPLETE SHORT STORIES OF ERNEST HEMINGWAY 29–30 (Finca Vigía ed., Simon & Schuster 1998).

37 DIANA B. HENRIQUES, THE WIZARD OF LIES: BERNIE MADOFF AND THE DEATH OF TRUST 33 (Times Books 2011).

38 AMY GOLDSTEIN, JANESVILLE: AN AMERICAN STORY 3 (2017).

39 HAN KANG, HUMAN ACTS 142 (Deborah Smith trans., 2017).

40 Sharon Peters, *Why We Should Listen to Dolphin "Voices,"* USA TODAY (Aug. 15, 2015, 2:02 PM), https://www.usatoday.com/story/life/books/2015/08/14/voices---ocean--journey-into--wild-and-haunting-world--dolphins/31117993/.

40 Philip Hoare, *Voices in the Ocean: A Journey into the Wild and Haunting World of Dolphins by Susan Casey*, GUARDIAN (Sept. 9, 2015, 05:29 AM), https://www.theguardian.com/books/2015/sep/09/voices-in-the-ocean-journey-into-wild-haunting-dolphins-susan-casey.

40 SUSAN CASEY, VOICES IN THE OCEAN 23 (2015).

Five

41 SALMAN RUSHDIE, THE GOLDEN HOUSE 340 (2017).

41 GABRIEL GARCÍA MÁRQUEZ, ONE HUNDRED YEARS OF SOLITUDE 86 (Harper Collins 2003).

42 TONI MORRISON, GOD HELP THE CHILD 73 (2015).

42 IMBOLO MBUE, BEHOLD THE DREAMERS 19 (2016).

42 *Id.* at 45.

43 DAVID GRANN, THE DEVIL AND SHERLOCK HOLMES: TALES OF MURDER, MADNESS AND OBSESSION 288–89 (2010).

NOTES

43 Jeane J. Kirkpatrick, *Dictatorships and Double Standards*, AM. ENTER. INST. (Nov. 1, 1979), http://www.aei.org/articles/dictatorships-and-double-standards-2/.
43 J. M. BARRIE, PETER PAN 102 (Kingman Books 2016).
43 WILLIAM SHAKESPEARE, A MIDSUMMER NIGHT'S DREAM 79 (Barbara A. Mowat & Paul Werstine eds., Simon & Schuster 2004).
44 *Bush v. Gore*, 531 U.S. 98, 155 (2000) (Breyer, J., dissenting).
44 T. J. STILES, THE FIRST TYCOON: THE EPIC LIFE OF CORNELIUS VANDERBILT 218 (2009).
44 RON CHERNOW, WASHINGTON: A LIFE 451 (2010).
44 EDMUND BURKE, 3 SELECT WORKS OF EDMUND BURKE 126–27 (Francis Canavan ed., Liberty Fund Payne 1975).
45 H. MONTGOMERY HYDE, THE TRIALS OF OSCAR WILDE 236 (1948).
46 Jelani Cobb, *Under Trump, a Hard Test for Howard University*, NEW YORKER (Jan. 15, 2018), https://www.newyorker.com/magazine/2018/01/15/under-trump-a-hard-test-for-howard-university.
47 NIALL FERGUSON, KISSINGER: 1923–1968: THE IDEALIST 1 (2015).
47 WALTER ISAACSON, KISSINGER: A BIOGRAPHY 451 (2005).
47 ROBERT DALLEK, NIXON AND KISSINGER: PARTNERS IN POWER 259 (2007).
48 HENRY KISSINGER, YEARS OF UPHEAVAL (Simon & Schuster 1982).

Six

49 JANET TODD, THE CAMBRIDGE INTRODUCTION TO JANE AUSTEN 1 (Cambridge University Press 2006).
50 EZRA POUND, LETTERS FROM EZRA POUND 308 (D. D. Paige ed., 1950).
50 JANE AUSTEN, THE COMPLETE NOVELS xi (Penguin Classics 2006). I am grateful to Syrie James for collecting and publishing an assortment of other writers praising Austen's work. My favorite is William Buckley Jr.'s insistence that "one doesn't read Jane Austen; one re-reads Jane Austen." For the full list, see http://www.syriejames.com/famousquotes-j.php.
51 Jane Austen, *Emma*, in THE COMPLETE NOVELS 829 (Wordsworth Editions 2007) (1815).
51 JANE AUSTEN, MANSFIELD PARK 6 (Ian Littlewood ed., Wordsworth Editions 2000) (1815).
51 JANE AUSTEN, PERSUASION 275 (Little, Brown 1899) (1817).

NOTES

51 Jane Austen, *Emma, in* THE COMPLETE NOVELS 791 (Wordsworth Editions 2007) (1815).

51 Jane Austen, *Sense and Sensibility, in* THE COMPLETE NOVELS 9 (Wordsworth Editions 2007) (1811).

52 Jane Austen, *Northanger Abbey, in* THE COMPLETE NOVELS 1084 (Wordsworth Editions 2007) (1817).

52 Jane Austen, *Pride and Prejudice, in* THE COMPLETE NOVELS 374 (Wordsworth Editions 2007) (1813).

52 JANE AUSTEN, LADY SUSAN 20 (Dover 2005) (1871).

Seven

53 JON MEACHAM, DESTINY AND POWER: THE AMERICAN ODYSSEY OF GEORGE HERBERT WALKER BUSH 39 (2015).

53 BRIAN GREENE, THE HIDDEN REALITY: PARALLEL UNIVERSES AND THE DEEP LAWS OF THE COSMOS 5 (2011).

54 AZAR NAFISI, THINGS I'VE BEEN SILENT ABOUT 56 (2008).

54 Ruth Franklin, *How Writing "My Struggle" Undid Knausgaard*, ATLANTIC (Nov. 2018), https://www.theatlantic.com/magazine/archive/2018/11/knausgaard-devours-himself/570847/.

55 TILAR J. MAZZEO, IRENA'S CHILDREN: THE EXTRAORDINARY STORY OF THE WOMAN WHO SAVED 2,500 CHILDREN FROM THE WARSAW GHETTO xii (2017).

55 GRAEME WOOD, THE WAY OF THE STRANGERS: ENCOUNTERS WITH THE ISLAMIC STATE 117 (2016).

55 JORGE LUIS BORGES, THE GARDEN OF FORKING PATHS 94 (Anthony Kerrigan trans., 1941).

55 DAN BARBER, THE THIRD PLATE: FIELD NOTES ON THE FUTURE OF FOOD 197 (2014).

56 JILL LEOVY, GHETTOSIDE: A TRUE STORY OF MURDER IN AMERICA 9 (2015).

56 HERMAN MELVILLE, BILLY BUDD, SAILOR 112 (Tom Doherty Associates 1992).

56 WILLIAM COHAN, THE LAST TYCOONS: THE SECRET HISTORY OF LAZARD FRÈRES & CO. 14 (2007).

56 WILLIAM FAULKNER, SANCTUARY 121 (1931).

NOTES

56 Justin Torres, *The Way We Read Now*, in IT OCCURS TO ME THAT I AM AMERICAN 349 (2018).

57 CRISTINA HENRÍQUEZ, THE BOOK OF UNKNOWN AMERICANS: A NOVEL 186 (2014).

57 STEVE LOPEZ, THE SOLOIST: A LOST DREAM, AN UNLIKELY FRIENDSHIP, AND THE REDEMPTIVE POWER OF MUSIC 35 (2010).

58 DAVE SOBEL, THE GLASS UNIVERSE: HOW THE LADIES OF THE HARVARD OBSERVATORY TOOK THE MEASURE OF THE STARS 77 (2016).

58 NATHALIA HOLT, RISE OF THE ROCKET GIRLS: THE WOMEN WHO PROPELLED US, FROM MISSILES TO THE MOON TO MARS 96 (2016).

59 Justice Felix Frankfurter, *Youngstown Sheet & Tube Co v. Sawyer* (1952).

59 Jeffrey Rosen, *The Nation: Social Court; the Justice Who Came to Dinner*, N.Y. TIMES (Feb. 1, 2004), https://www.nytimes.com/2004/02/01/weekinreview/the-nation-social-court-the-justice-who-came-to-dinner.html.

60 KHALED HOSSEINI, THE KITE RUNNER 122 (2003).

60 *Id.* at 130.

Eight

61 Linda Johnson Rice, *CEO's Letter: The Class of 2017*, EBONY, Dec. 2017, at 14.

61 THOMAS L. DYJA, THE THIRD COAST: WHEN CHICAGO BUILT THE AMERICAN DREAM 25–26 (2013).

62 LISA KO, THE LEAVERS 214 (2017).

62 TOM REISS, THE BLACK COUNT: GLORY, REVOLUTION, AND THE REAL COUNT OF MONTE CRISTO 151 (2012).

63 SHONDA RHIMES, YEAR OF YES 262 (Simon & Schuster 2016).

63 FREDRIK BACKMAN, BEARTOWN 181 (Neil Smith trans., 2016).

63 WALTER ISAACSON, EINSTEIN: HIS LIFE AND UNIVERSE 52 (2007).

63 H. W. BRANDS, THE MAN WHO SAVED THE UNION: ULYSSES GRANT IN WAR AND PEACE 425 (2012).

64 A. SCOTT BERG, WILSON (2013).

64 Dan Chiasson, *"2001: A Space Odyssey": What It Means, and How It Was Made*, NEW YORKER (Apr. 23, 2018), https://www.newyorker.com/magazine/2018/04/23/2001-a-space-odyssey-what-it-means-and-how-it-was-made.

64 Ann Hornaday, *With "Detroit," Kathryn Bigelow Refines an Aesthetic Grounded in Equal Parts Theory and Reality*, WASH. POST (July 27, 2017), https://www.washingtonpost.com/lifestyle/style/with-detroit-kathryn-bigelow-refines-an-aesthetic-grounded-in-equal-parts-theory-and-reality/2017/07/26/c5c5f554-7206-11e7-8839-ec48ec4cae25_story.html?utm_term=.9bc76a1a931e.

64 Teresa Wiltz, *Equal Parts Blisters and Enlightenment*, WASH. POST (Aug. 9, 2006), http://www.washingtonpost.com/wp-dyn/content/article/2006/08/08/AR2006080801561.html.

64 Joseph Hess, *Equal Parts Idiocy and Idealism*, WASH. POST (July 8, 1989), https://www.washingtonpost.com/archive/opinions/1989/07/08/equal-parts-idiocy-and-idealism/97dcd381-21b7-47d8-ae6c-839cbe754fd7/?utm_term=.f96fe0b04adb.

64 Wajahat Ali, *A Muslim Among Israeli Settlers*, ATLANTIC (June 2018), https://www.theatlantic.com/magazine/archive/2018/06/a-muslim-among-the-settlers/559145/.

65 GARY RIVLIN, KATRINA: AFTER THE FLOOD 249 (Simon & Schuster 2016).

66 AMANDA PALMER, THE ART OF ASKING: HOW I LEARNED TO STOP WORRYING AND LET PEOPLE HELP 228 (reprint ed., Grand Central Publishing 2015).

67 Christian Alejandro Gonzalez, *Academia Needs Conservative Professors*, NAT'L REV. (June 27, 2018), https://www.nationalreview.com/2018/06/colleges-universities-need-conservative-professors/.

67 David M. Shapiro, *Guns, Speech, Charlottesville: The Semiotics of Semiautomatics*, 106 GEO L. J. ONLINE (2017), https://georgetownlawjournal.org/articles/244/commentary-guns-speech-charlottesville/pdf.

67 David Cole, *The Disgrace of Our Criminal Justice*, N.Y. REV. BOOKS (Dec. 4, 2014), https://www.nybooks.com/articles/2014/12/04/disgrace-our-criminal-justice/.

Nine

69 LEE FENNELL, SLICES AND LUMPS: DIVISION AND AGGREGATION IN LAW AND LIFE 2 (2019).

69 SY MONTGOMERY, THE SOUL OF AN OCTOPUS: A SURPRISING EXPLORATION INTO THE WONDER OF CONSCIOUSNESS 83 (2015).

70 JOSEPH ELLIS, AMERICAN CREATION 189 (2007).

70 JENNIFER EBERHARDT, BIASED 6 (2019).

70 James Forman Jr., Locking Up Our Own: Crime and Punishment in Black America 12 (2017).

71 Bart Ehrman, The Triumph of Christianity: How a Forbidden Religion Swept the World 16 (2018).

72 *Gray v. Sanders*, 372 U.S. 368, 381 (1963).

72 *McCulloch v. Maryland*, 17 U.S. 316, 408 (1819).

72 Anders Ericsson & Robert Pool, Peak: Secrets from the New Science of Expertise 176 (2016).

73 Taylor Branch, Parting the Waters: America in the King Years 1954–1963 195 (1988).

73 Bianca Bosker, *Mayonnaise, Disrupted*, Atlantic (Nov. 2017), https://www.theatlantic.com/magazine/archive/2017/11/hampton-creek-josh-tetrick-mayo-mogul/540642/.

73 Niall Ferguson, The Square and the Tower: Networks and Power, from the Freemasons to Facebook 106 (2017).

73 Jake Knapp & John Zeratsky, Make Time: How to Focus on What Matters Every Day (2018).

73 Barry Nalebuff & Ian Ayres, Why Not? How to Use Everyday Ingenuity to Solve Problems Big and Small 88 (2003).

74 I. Glenn Cohen, Harvard Law School, https://hls.harvard.edu/faculty/directory/10176/Cohen (last visited Jan. 20, 2020).

74 Benjamin J. Horwich, Munger, Tolles & Olsen, https://www.mto.com/lawyers/Benjamin-J-Horwich (last visited Jan. 20, 2020).

74 Paul Kalanithi, When Breath Becomes Air 99 (2016).

76 Mary Beard, Women and Power: A Manifesto (2017).

Ten

77 Saïd Sayrafiezadeh, *Audition*, New Yorker (Sept. 10, 2018), https://www.newyorker.com/magazine/2018/09/10/audition.

78 Daniel Tammet, Every Word Is a Bird We Teach to Sing 14 (2017).

78 Geoffrey R. Stone et al., Constitutional Law 75 (8th ed. 2017). The justices the quote refers to are those appointed by President Nixon: Chief Justice Burger and Justices Blackmun, Powell, and Rehnquist.

79 Matthew Cobb, *The Brave New World of Gene Editing*, N.Y. Rev. Books (July 13, 2017), https://www.nybooks.com/articles/2017/07/13/brave-new-world-of-gene-editing/.

80 Sebastian Rotella, *A Gunfight in Guatemala*, ProPublica (June 2, 2016), https://www.propublica.org/article/a-gunfight-in-guatemala.
80 Jeffrey Toobin, American Heiress: The Wild Saga of the Kidnapping, Crimes, and Trial of Patty Hearst 143 (reprint ed., Anchor Books 2016).
80 Milan Kundera, The Unbearable Lightness of Being 155 (Michael Henry Heim trans., 1994).
80 Morten Hansen, Great at Work: How Top Performers Do Less, Work Better, and Achieve More 34 (2018).
80 Tony Hsieh, Delivering Happiness 182 (reprint ed., Grand Central Publishing 2013).
81 *Cheney v. United States District Court for the District of Columbia*, 542 U.S. 367, 386 (2004).
81 James McBride, Song Yet Sung 294 (reprint ed., Riverhead Books 2008).
81 Ruth Franklin, Shirley Jackson: A Rather Haunted Life 423 (2016).
81 J. D. Vance, Hillbilly Elegy 85 (reprint ed., HarperCollins 2016).
82 Alex Hutchinson, Endure: Mind, Body, and the Curiously Elastic Limits of Human Performance 10 (2018).
82 *Id.* at 142.
83 Amanda Ripley, The Smartest Kids in the World 268 (2013).
84 John Bogle, The Little Book of Common Sense Investing (2007).
84 Gerald N. Rosenberg, The Hollow Hope: Can Courts Bring About Social Change? 157 (2d ed. 2008).
84 Pope Francis, The Name of God Is Mercy 77 (Oonagh Stransky trans., 2016).

Eleven

85 Zadie Smith, White Teeth 251 (2000).
85 Washington Irving, The Legend of Sleepy Hollow 13–14 (Cosimo 2007) (1820).
86 Rachel Carson, Silent Spring 219 (1962).
86 Milton Friedman, Capitalism and Freedom 25 (1962).
86 Simon Winchester, The Map That Changed the World: William Smith and the Birth of Modern Geology 39 (2001).

Notes

87 John Phillip Santos, *Américo Paredes vs. J. Frank Dobie*, Texas Monthly (Sept. 18, 2019), https://www.texasmonthly.com/articles/americo-paredes-j-frank-dobie/.

87 Reinhold Niebuhr, *The Atomic Issue*, Christianity & Crisis (Oct. 15, 1945), at 7.

87 Gordon S. Wood, Friends Divided: John Adams and Thomas Jefferson 431 (2017).

88 Adam Grant, Originals: How Non-Conformists Move the World 5 (2016).

88 Theodore Roethke, *Vernal Sentiment*, New Yorker (Mar. 30, 1904), at 65.

88 Jhumpa Lahiri, In Other Words 25 (Ann Goldstein trans., 2015).

88 Jonathan Safran Foer, Here I Am 162 (2016).

89 Henry Marsh, Do No Harm: Stories of Life, Death, and Brain Surgery 5 (2014).

89 Joan Didion, Slouching Towards Bethlehem (1968).

89 *Hammer v. Dagenhart*, 247 U.S. 251, 277 (1918), overruled in part by *United States v. Darby*, 312 U.S. 100 (1941).

89 *Carter v. Carter Coal Co.*, 298 U.S. 238, 309 (1936).

90 *United States v. Lopez*, 514 U.S. 549, 561 (1995).

90 *Lockhart v. United States*, 136 S. Ct. 958, 972 (2016).

91 David Ogilvy, Confessions of an Advertising Man 75 (1963).

91 St. Augustine, The Confessions of St. Augustine (Edward Bouverie Busey trans., Project Gutenberg 2002) (400 CE), https://www.gutenberg.org/files/3296/3296-h/3296-h.htm.

92 William Styron, The Confessions of Nat Turner 155 (1967).

93 *Korematsu v. U.S.*, 323 U.S. 214, 240 (1944), abrogated by *Trump v. Hawaii*, 138 S. Ct. 2392 (2018).

94 Max Hastings, Inferno: The World at War, 1939–1945 5 (2011).

94 Winston S. Churchill, Memoirs of the Second World War 5 (1948).

94 *Winston Churchill Facts*, Nobel Prize, https://www.nobelprize.org/prizes/literature/1953/churchill/facts/ (last visited Apr. 25, 2019).

Twelve

95 Kathryn J. Edin & H. Luke Shaefer, $2.00 a Day: Living on Almost Nothing in America xi (2015).

Notes

95 Victoria Johnson, American Eden: David Hosack, Botany, and Medicine in the Garden of the Early Republic 1 (2018).
96 Walter Isaacson, Leonardo da Vinci 276 (2017).
96 Tara Westover, Educated: A Memoir 328 (2018).
98 Wesley Morris, *Rom-Coms Were Corny and Retrograde. Why Do I Miss Them So Much?*, N.Y. Times Mag. (Apr. 24, 2019), https://www.nytimes.com/2019/04/24/magazine/romantic-comedy-movies.html.
99 Henry Louis Gates Jr., Stony the Road: Reconstruction, White Supremacy, and the Rise of Jim Crow 227 (2019).
99 Ann Patchett, Bel Canto 18 (2008).
99 Steven Pinker, The Stuff of Thought: Language as a Window into Human Nature 354 (2005).
100 Thomas L. Friedman, Thank You for Being Late: An Optimist's Guide to Thriving in the Age of Accelerations 3 (2016).
100 Jon Krakauer, Missoula: Rape and the Justice System in a College Town 131–32 (2015).
100 Heidi Grant Halvorson & E. Tory Higgins, Focus (2013).
101 Hari Kunzru, White Tears 19 (2017).
101 Katherine Bell, *The Ideas That Shaped Management in 2013*, Harv. Bus. Rev. (Dec. 24, 2013), https://hbr.org/2013/12/the-ideas-that-shaped-management-in-2013.
101 Susan David, Emotional Agility: Get Unstuck, Embrace Change, and Thrive in Work and Life 3 (2016).
102 Amy Poehler, Yes Please 19 (2015).

Thirteen

104 W. W. Norton & Co., The Norton Anthology of African American Literature (Henry Louis Gates Jr. et al. eds., 3d ed. 2014).
104 Therman O'Daniel, *James Baldwin: An Interpretive Study*, 7 C. Language Ass'n J. 37, 38 (1963).
104 Darryl Pinckney, *On James Baldwin*, N.Y. Rev. Books (Apr. 4, 2013), https://www.nybooks.com/articles/2013/04/04/james-baldwin/.
104 *Id.*
105 James Baldwin, Notes of a Native Son 52 (rev. ed. 2012).
105 James Baldwin, *As Much Truth as One Can Bear*, N.Y. Times (Jan. 14, 1962), at BR11.

NOTES

106 James Baldwin, The Fire Next Time 31 (1992).

106 James Baldwin, *If Black English Isn't a Language, Then Tell Me, What Is?*, 27 Black Scholar 5, 5 (1979).

106 James Baldwin, Notes of a Native Son 117–18 (1955).

106 James Baldwin, *The Crusade of Indignation*, Nation (Apr. 12, 2011), https://www.thenation.com/article/crusade-indignation/.

106 Baldwin, *supra* note 8 at xxxii.

Fourteen

107 Alexis de Tocqueville, Democracy in America 316 (Arthur Goldhammer trans., Library of America 2004) (1835).

107 David Bianculli, The Platinum Age of Television: From I Love Lucy to The Walking Dead, How TV Became Terrific 198 (2016).

108 Lizzie Widdicombe, *Parenting by the Numbers*, New Yorker (May 27, 2019), https://www.newyorker.com/magazine/2019/06/03/parenting-by-the-numbers.

108 Adam Winkler, We the Corporations: How American Businesses Won Their Civil Rights 302 (2018).

108 Erik Brynjolfsson & Andrew McAfee, The Second Machine Age: Work, Progress, and Prosperity in a Time of Brilliant Technologies 7–8 (2016).

109 Philip Larkin, Required Writing: Miscellaneous Pieces, 1955–1982 8 (1983).

109 Paul Collins, *Has Modern Life Killed the Semicolon?*, Music & Culture (June 20, 2008), http://musicandculture.blogspot.com/2008/06/has-modern-life-killed-semicolon.html.

109 Michael Moss, Salt Sugar Fat: How the Food Giants Hooked Us 114 (2013).

109 Stephen C. Yeazell & Joanna C. Schwartz, Civil Procedure 529 (10th ed. 2018).

110 Jill Lepore, *Baby Doe: A Political History of Tragedy*, New Yorker (Jan. 24, 2016), https://www.newyorker.com/magazine/2016/02/01/baby-doe.

110 Michael J. Sandel, Justice: What's the Right Thing to Do? 89 (2008).

110 Angela Duckworth, Grit: The Power of Passion and Perseverance 72 (2016).

110 HOME RECORDING OF COPYRIGHTED WORKS: HEARINGS BEFORE THE SUBCOMM. ON COURTS, CIVIL LIBERTIES, & THE ADMIN. OF JUSTICE, 97TH CONG. 8 (1983) (statement of Jack Valenti, President, Motion Picture Association of America, Inc.), https://hdl.handle.net/2027/mdp.39015082326862.

111 Pedro Ponce, *The Imperfect Eye of Edward Curtis*, HUMAN. (May/June 2000), at 38.

111 TIMOTHY EGAN, SHORT NIGHTS OF THE SHADOW CATCHER: THE EPIC LIFE AND IMMORTAL PHOTOGRAPHS OF EDWARD CURTIS 106 (2013).

112 Paul Graham, *The Refragmentation*, PAUL GRAHAM (Jan. 2016), http://paulgraham.com/re.html.

112 HENRY FORD, MY LIFE AND WORK xxv (2008).

113 *Patent Series—Caveat Files: Case 110: Motion Pictures (1888)*, THOMAS A. EDISON PAPERS RUTGERS U., http://edison.rutgers.edu/NamesSearch/SingleDoc.php?DocId=PT031AAA1 (last visited July 20, 2019).

Fifteen

115 EUGENE ROGAN, THE ARABS: A HISTORY 39 (2009).

116 PETER GODFREY-SMITH, OTHER MINDS: THE OCTOPUS, THE SEA, AND THE DEEP ORIGINS OF CONSCIOUSNESS 17 (2016).

116 ALBERT MARRIN, UPROOTED: THE JAPANESE AMERICAN EXPERIENCE DURING WORLD WAR II 7 (2016).

118 SHERMAN ALEXIE, YOU DON'T HAVE TO SAY YOU LOVE ME: A MEMOIR 87 (2017).

118 JOSE ANTONIO VARGAS, DEAR AMERICA: NOTES OF AN UNDOCUMENTED CITIZEN 23 (2018).

118 *Gonzales v. Raich*, 545 U.S. 1, 53 (2005) (O'Connor, J., dissenting).

118 JOHN IRVING, THE WORLD ACCORDING TO GARP 230 (1978).

118 ALICE MUNRO, TOO MUCH HAPPINESS (2009).

119 STEPHEN HAWKING & LEONARD MLODINOW, THE GRAND DESIGN (2010).

119 TOM WOLFE, THE KINGDOM OF SPEECH (2016).

119 JULIAN BARNES, FLAUBERT'S PARROT 39 (1984).

119 SEBASTIAN JUNGER, WAR 43 (2010).

120 NORA EPHRON, THE MOST OF NORA EPHRON 390 (2013).

NOTES

121 Alex Tizon, *In the Land of Missing Persons*, ATLANTIC (Apr. 2016), https://www.theatlantic.com/magazine/archive/2016/04/in-the-land-of-missing-persons/471477/.

121 Jodi Cash, *Leveling the Field for Family Farms*, THE BITTER SOUTHERNER (2017), https://bittersoutherner.com/leveling-the-field-for-family-farms-wendell-berry-institute?rq=Leveling%20the%20Field%20for%20Family%20Farms.

121 Ben Schachter, *Forgetful Architecture*, COMMENTARY (Oct. 19, 2010), https://www.commentarymagazine.com/culture-civilization/art/forgetful-architecture/.

121 Jessica Pishko, *The FBI Accused Him of Terrorism. He Couldn't Tie His Shoes*, ESQUIRE (Sept. 8, 2016), https://www.esquire.com/news-politics/a47390/alabama-isis-peyton-pruitt/.

121 Megan Rose & ProPublica, *The Deal Prosecutors Offer When They Have No Cards Left to Play*, ATLANTIC (Sept. 7, 2017), https://www.theatlantic.com/politics/archive/2017/09/what-does-an-innocent-man-have-to-do-to-go-free-plead-guilty/539001/.

Sixteen

123 ISABEL WILKERSON, THE WARMTH OF OTHER SUNS: THE EPIC STORY OF AMERICA'S GREAT MIGRATION 10 (2010).

124 Robin Niblett, *Liberalism in Retreat: The Demise of a Dream*, FOREIGN AFFAIRS (Jan.–Feb. 2017), https://www.foreignaffairs.com/articles/2016-12-12/liberalism-retreat.

124 Anna Güntner, Konstantin Lucks, & Julia Sperling-Magro, *Lessons from the Front Line of Corporate Nudging*, MCKINSEY QUARTERLY (Jan. 2019), https://www.mckinsey.com/business-functions/organization/our-insights/lessons-from-the-front-line-of-corporate-nudging.

125 LUCY COOKE, THE TRUTH ABOUT ANIMALS: STONED SLOTHS, LOVELORN HIPPOS, AND OTHER TALES FROM THE WILD SIDE OF WILDLIFE 267 (2018).

126 STEVEN PINKER, ENLIGHTENMENT NOW: THE CASE FOR REASON, SCIENCE, HUMANISM, AND PROGRESS 122 (2018).

126 SETH STEPHENS-DAVIDOWITZ, EVERYBODY LIES: BIG DATA, NEW DATA, AND WHAT THE INTERNET CAN TELL US ABOUT WHO WE REALLY ARE 211 (2017).

126 Nathaniel Rich, *The Most Honest Book About Climate Change Yet*, Atlantic: Sci. (Oct. 2018), https://www.theatlantic.com/magazine/archive/2018/10/william-vollmann-carbon-ideologies/568309/.

126 Pankaj Mishra, *The Great Protester*, New Yorker (Oct. 22, 2018), at 82.

127 James Mattis, "The Enemy Within", Atlantic: Ideas (Dec. 2019), https://www.theatlantic.com/magazine/archive/2019/12/james-mattis-the-enemy-within/600781/.

127 Dan Chiasson, *"2001: A Space Odyssey": What It Means, and How It Was Made*, New Yorker (Apr. 23, 2018), https://www.newyorker.com/magazine/2018/04/23/2001-a-space-odyssey-what-it-means-and-how-it-was-made.

127 Neil Shubin, Your Inner Fish: A Journey into the 3.5-Billion-Year History of the Human Body 110 (2008).

127 Ed Yong, I Contain Multitudes: The Microbes Within Us and a Grander View of Life 151 (2016).

128 Eva Gudbergsdottir, *Institute MA TESOL Program Receives U.S. State Department Award*, Middlebury Institute Int'l Stud. Monterey (Dec. 3, 2019), https://www.middlebury.edu/institute/news/institute-ma-tesol-program-receives-us-state-department-award. The original sentence seemed to have a grammatical error (or a least a typo) in it. It contained a comma splice: "The Institute has a long history of alumni who become English Language Fellows, in fact, since 2006, 32 MATESOL alumni have served as ELFs around the world in countries as diverse as Moldova, Rwanda, Thailand, and Brazil." So I inserted a semicolon. I also dropped the "MATESOL" acronym since that might not be familiar to general readers. A similar concern motivated my switching "served as ELFs" to "served as [fellows]."

128 Jennifer Bann & John Corbett, Spelling Scots: The Orthography of Literary Scots, 1700–2000 140 (2015).

129 *About "From Our Own Correspondent,"* BBC Radio 4: From Our Own Correspondent, https://www.bbc.co.uk/programmes/articles/53vWLpCZFgdvs4C939jcLGv/about-from-our-own-correspondent.

129 Bruce Springsteen, Born to Run 135 (2016).

131 Questlove, Creative Quest 192 (2018).

Notes

Seventeen

133 Robert K. Massie, Catherine the Great: Portrait of a Woman 21 (2011).

133 *Boumediene v. Bush*, 553 U.S. 723, 729 (2008).

134 Atul Gawande, Being Mortal 115 (2014).

134 Joy Williams, *Chaunt*, New Yorker (Dec 10, 2018), https://www.newyorker.com/magazine/2018/12/10/chaunt.

135 Karen Russell, *The New Veterans*, Granta (Jan. 13, 2013), https://granta.com/the-new-veterans/.

135 Tracy Kidder, A Truck Full of Money 15 (2016). Kidder includes a paragraph break after the quotation that ends with "I'm quite good at hiring." But that created some awkward spacing when including the passage in this book. So I got rid of the break. A similar reason drove me to shorten the subtitle of the book to just "The Life of an American Entrepreneur." You can find the full name, however, in the citation.

135 David France, How to Survive a Plague: The Inside Story of How Citizens and Science Tamed AIDS 14 (2016).

135 Bernhard Schlink, The Reader 29 (Carol Brown Janeway trans., 1995).

136 Susan Dunn, *Eleanor in War and Love*, N.Y. Rev. Books (Dec. 8, 2016), https://web.williams.edu/humanities/sdunn/articles/EleanorinWarandLove.pdf.

136 David Maraniss, Once in a Great City: A Detroit Story 225 (2015).

136 Michael Specter, *The Gene Hackers*, New Yorker (Nov. 8, 2015), https://www.newyorker.com/magazine/2015/11/16/the-gene-hackers.

137 Barbara Tuchman, The Proud Tower: A Portrait of the World before the War, 1890–1914 184 (1966).

138 Sylvia Nasar, A Beautiful Mind 175 (2011).

139 Richard Panek, The 4% Universe: Dark Matter, Dark Energy, and the Race to Discover the Rest of Reality 6 (2011). The full quote includes a second use of "more than," though not one that uses alliteration: "Cosmology was where old astronomers went to die. It was more philosophy than physics, more speculation than investigation." *Id.*

139 Susan Faludi, In the Darkroom 265 (2016).

140 David Pierce, *Inside Andy Rubin's Quest to Create an OS for Everything*, Wired (July 25, 2017), https://www.wired.com/story/inside-andy-rubins-quest-to-create-an-os-for-everything/.

Eighteen

141 Eric Konigsberg, *The Billionaire Battle in the Bahamas*, Vanity Fair (Dec. 6, 2015), https://www.vanityfair.com/news/2015/12/peter-nygard-louis-bacon-legal-battle-bahamas.

141 Margot Lee Shetterly, Hidden Figures: The American Dream and the Untold Story of the Black Women Mathematicians Who Helped Win the Space Race 191–92 (2016).

142 Allie Rowbottom, Jell-O Girls: A Family History 17 (2018).

142 Tessa Hadley, *The Bunty Club*, New Yorker (Oct. 28, 2019), https://www.newyorker.com/magazine/2019/10/28/the-bunty-club.

143 Ron Chernow, The House of Morgan: An American Banking Dynasty and the Rise of Modern Finance 258 (2010).

143 Deborah Blum, The Poison Squad: One Chemist's Single-Minded Crusade for Food Safety at the Turn of the Twentieth Century 26 (2018).

143 Madeline Miller, Circe 6 (2018).

144 Richard Russo, Bridge of Sighs 73 (2007).

144 Jeffrey Rosen, "Google's Gatekeepers", N.Y. Times (Nov. 1, 2008), https://www.nytimes.com/2008/12/01/technology/01iht-01google.18308416.html.

144 Garth Risk Hallberg, City on Fire 129 (2015).

144 David Blight, Frederick Douglass: Prophet of Freedom 80 (2018).

145 William Styron, Darkness Visible 31 (1989).

145 Mark Jacobson, *65*, N.Y. Mag. (Apr. 4, 2014), https://nymag.com/news/features/middle-old-age-2014-4/.

145 Anthony Bourdain, Kitchen Confidential 66 (2000).

145 Allen Guelzo, Gettysburg 328 (2013).

146 Candice Millard, Hero of the Empire: The Boer War, a Daring Escape, and the Making of Winston Churchill 8 (2018).

147 "George Kennan's 'Long Telegram'", February 22, 1946. https://digitalarchive.wilsoncenter.org/document/116178.pdf

148 Haruki Murakami, Killing Commendatore (2017).

148 Haruki Murakami, Blind Willow, Sleeping Woman 201 (2006).

148 Haruki Murakami, *Samsa in Love*, New Yorker (Oct. 21, 2013), https://www.newyorker.com/magazine/2013/10/28/samsa-in-love.

148 *Id.*

148 Haruki Murakami, *Drive My Car*, in Men Without Women 1 (2017).
148 *Id.* at 5.

Nineteen

149 George W. Bush, *Statement by the President on the Death of William F. Buckley, Jr.*, C-SPAN (Oct. 6, 2005), https://www.c-span.org/video/?189223-1/tribute-william-f-buckley.
150 Marshall Loeb, *Bill Buckley, Liberals' Favorite Conservative*, MarketWatch (Feb. 27, 2008, 6:38 PM), https://www.marketwatch.com/story/bill-buckley-liberals-favorite-conservative.
150 *Id.*
150 William F. Buckley Jr., Saving the Queen 20 (2005).
150 *Id.* at 54.
150 *Id.* at 72.
151 *Id.* at 61.
152 William F. Buckley Jr., God and Man at Yale xxxii (1951).
152 William F. Buckley Jr., Nearer, My God: An Autobiography of Faith 64 (1997).
152 William F. Buckley Jr., Up from Liberalism (1959).
152 William F. Buckley Jr., Brothers No More 123 (1995)
153 William F. Buckley Jr., Saving the Queen, acknowledgments (1976).

Twenty

155 Jeffrey Toobin, The Oath: The Obama White House and the Supreme Court 90 (2012).
155 Yann Martel, Beatrice and Virgil 189 (2010).
156 Agatha Christie, The Mysterious Affair at Styles 3 (1920).
156 Arthur Hobson Quinn, Edgar Allan Poe: A Critical Biography 83 (1997).
157 *Id.* at 39.
157 Alfred Owen Aldridge, Benjamin Franklin: Philosopher & Man 43 (1965).
158 Michael Specter, *Freedom from Fries*, New Yorker (Nov. 2, 2015), https://www.newyorker.com/magazine/2015/11/02/freedom-from-fries.

NOTES

158 David Foster Wallace, Infinite Jest 166 (1996).

158 Jeffrey Eugenides, Middlesex 166 (2002).

158 Maya Angelou, *Eulogy for Coretta Scott King* (Feb. 7, 2006), https://awpc.cattcenter.iastate.edu/2017/03/21/remarks-at-the-funeral-service-for-coretta-scott-king-feb-7-2006/.

158 Henry James, The Wings of the Dove 48 (1913).

159 Hannah Arendt, The Origins of Totalitarianism 189 (1951).

160 Tom Wolfe, The Bonfire of the Vanities 143 (1987).

160 Jane Smiley, Private Life 281 (2010).

161 Jon Landau, *Sticky Fingers*, Rolling Stone: Album Reviews (Apr. 23, 1971), https://www.rollingstone.com/music/music-album-reviews/sticky-fingers-107725/.

Twenty-One

163 Alex Haley, Roots: The Saga of an American Family 207 (2007).

163 Roger Lowenstein, When Genius Failed: The Rise and Fall of Long-Term Capital Management 151 (2000).

164 Jianying Zha, *Constance Wu's Hollywood Destiny*, New Yorker (Sept. 16, 2019), https://www.newyorker.com/magazine/2019/09/23/constance-wus-hollywood-destiny.

165 Imbolo Mbue, Behold the Dreamers 34 (2016).

165 A. J. Jacobs, The Year of Living Biblically: One Man's Quest to Follow the Bible as Literally as Possible 98 (2007).

165 Anthony Trollope, The Duke's Children 52 (1912).

165 Sigrid Nunez, The Friend 211 (2018).

166 Andrew Sullivan, *I Used to Be a Human Being*, N.Y. Mag. (Sept. 19, 2016), http://nymag.com/intelligencer/2016/09/andrew-sullivan-my-distraction-sickness-and-yours.html.

166 Alice Gregory, *Lessons from the Last Swiss Finishing School*, New Yorker (Oct. 8, 2018), https://www.newyorker.com/magazine/2018/10/08/lessons-from-the-last-swiss-finishing-school.

166 David Grann, *Stealing Time*, New Yorker (Sept. 5, 2005), https://www.newyorker.com/magazine/2005/09/12/stealing-time-2.

167 Louis Menand, *What Personality Tests Really Deliver*, New Yorker (Sept. 10, 2018), https://www.newyorker.com/magazine/2018/09/10/what-personality-tests-really-deliver.

167	Bharat Anand, The Content Trap: A Strategist's Guide to Digital Change xvii (2016).
167	Tim Flannery, *The Big Melt*, N.Y. Rev. Books (Aug. 16, 2018), https://www.nybooks.com/articles/2018/08/16/arctic-big-melt/.
168	David W. Blight: Books, http://www.davidwblight.com/books (last visited Mar. 26, 2019).
168	David W. Blight, Frederick Douglass: Prophet of Freedom xvi (2018).
168	*Id.* at 177.
168	*Id.* at 518.
169	*Id.* at 251.
169	Frederick Douglass, My Bondage and My Freedom 420 (University of South Florida ed. 2000) (1855), https://docsouth.unc.edu/neh/douglass55/douglass55.html (last visited Mar. 26, 2019).
170	Jill Leovy, Ghettoside: A True Story of Murder in America 40 (2015).
170	William Thackeray, Vanity Fair: A Novel without a Hero 27 (1848).

Twenty-Two

171	Adam Alter, Irresistible: The Rise of Addictive Technology and the Business of Keeping Us Hooked 82 (2017).
171	Andrew Solomon, Far from the Tree: Parents, Children, and the Search for Identity 74 (2012).
172	Created in 1986 by the English illustrator Martin Handford, the series is known as *Where's Wally?* in Britain. The name was changed to *Where's Waldo?* when it was later published in North America.
172	Kathryn Schulz, Being Wrong: Adventures in the Margin of Error 41 (2010).
173	Adam Lashinsky, Inside Apple: How America's Most Admired—and Secretive—Company Really Works 93 (2012).
173	Tilar J. Mazzeo, Irena's Children: The Extraordinary Story of the Woman Who Saved 2,500 Children from the Warsaw Ghetto 45 (2017).
173	Curtis Sittenfeld, American Wife 54 (2009).
175	Alice Waters, Coming to My Senses: The Making of a Counterculture Cook 27 (2017).

175 Arnold Rampersad, Ralph Ellison: A Biography 159 (2007).

175 Trevor Noah, Born a Crime 65 (2016).

175 Yascha Mounk, *How a Teen's Death Has Become a Political Weapon*, New Yorker (Jan. 21, 2019), https://www.newyorker.com/magazine/2019/01/28/how-a-teens-death-has-become-a-political-weapon.

176 Gary Klein, Seeing What Others Don't: The Remarkable Ways We Gain Insights 6 (2013).

176 Adam Gopnik, *How the Man of Reason Got Radicalized*, New Yorker (Feb. 25, 2019), https://www.newyorker.com/magazine/2019/03/04/how-the-man-of-reason-got-radicalized.

176 Daniel Coyle, The Talent Code: Greatness Isn't Born. It's Grown. Here's How 101 (2009).

176 David Baron, American Eclipse 48 (2017).

177 Judith Shulevitz, *Why You Never See Your Friends Anymore*, Atlantic (Nov. 2019), https://www.theatlantic.com/magazine/archive/2019/11/why-dont-i-see-you-anymore/598336/.

177 Andrei Hagiu & Julian Wright, *When Data Creates Competitive Advantage*, Harv. Bus. Rev. (Jan.–Feb. 2020), https://hbr.org/2020/01/when-data-creates-competitive-advantage.

178 David A. Kessler, Capture: Unraveling the Mystery of Mental Suffering 20–28, 70–72, 83–86, 99–111 (2016).

178 *Id.* at 266.

179 H. W. Brands, The General vs. the President: MacArthur and Truman at the Brink of Nuclear War 63 (2016).

180 David Saville Muzzey, Thomas Jefferson 185 (1918).

180 Lauren Collins, *India Mahdavi, Virtuosos of Color*, New Yorker (Mar. 12, 2018), https://www.newyorker.com/magazine/2018/03/19/india-mahdavi-virtuoso-of-color.

Twenty-Three

181 Samuel Johnson, Lives of the Poets: Addison, Savage, and Swift 41 (Outlook Verlag 2018) (1779).

182 Richard Frank & Sherry Glied, Better But Not Well 3 (2006).

182 Gerald Klerman, *Better But Not Well: Social and Ethical Issues in the Deinstitutionalization of the Mentally Ill*, 3 Schizophrenia Bulletin 617, 628 (1997), https://academic.oup.com/schizophreniabulletin/article/3/4/617/1892874.

NOTES

183 Carl Jung, Archetypes and the Collective Unconscious 156 (Gerhard Adler & R. F. C. Hull eds., trans., Princeton University Press 1969).
184 E. M. Forster, Howards End 107 (1910).
184 Penelope Fitzgerald, *At Hiruharama, in* The Means of Escape 113 (2000).
184 Mohsin Hamid, Exit West 180 (2017).
184 Michael Chabon, Moonglow 419 (2016).
184 Margaret Atwood, Hag-Seed: William Shakespeare's The Tempest Retold 34 (2016).
185 Charles Beaumont, Perchance to Dream 1 (1958).
186 Mary Roach, Stiff: The Curious Lives of Human Cadavers 116 (2003).
187 David Sedaris, *Santaland Diaries, in* Barrel Fever: Stories and Essays 186 (1994).
188 F. Scott Fitzgerald, *The Lees of Happiness* 5 (1922).
189 Yuval Levin, *Yuval Levin on Commentary*, Commentary (Dec. 29, 2015), https://www.commentarymagazine.com/culture-civilization/yuval-levin-on-commentarys-dazzling-balancing-act/.

Twenty-Four

191 Bharat Anand, The Content Trap: A Strategist's Guide to Digital Change 196 (2016). Anand offers an illuminating case study of *The Economist* and its interesting approach to online content. He compares it, in helpful ways, to the very different approach taking by the Norwegian media conglomerate Schibsted. You can find this analysis in a chapter Anand calls "A Digital Contrast." Earlier in the book, Anand also looks at the online strategy taken by the *New York Times*. You can find that in the chapter called "The *New York Times* Paywall."
194 *Fears of British English's Disappearance Are Overblown*, Economist (July 20, 2018), https://www.economist.com/books-and-arts/2017/07/20/fears-of-british-englishs-disappearance-are-overblown.
194 *Glencore's Attempt at Reinventing Mining Has Run into Trouble*, Economist (Dec. 1, 2018), https://www.economist.com/business/2018/12/01/glencores-attempt-at-reinventing-mining-has-run-into-trouble.
194 *How Will Imran Khan Govern?*, Economist (Aug. 2, 2018), https://www.economist.com/asia/2018/08/02/how-will-imran-khan-govern.

NOTES

194 *The Spotlight Shifts from Germany to France*, Economist (Sept. 30, 2017), https://www.economist.com/leaders/2017/09/30/the-spotlight-shifts-from-germany-to-france.

194 *The Truth about a No-Deal Brexit*, Economist (Nov. 24, 2018), https://www.economist.com/leaders/2018/11/24/the-truth-about-a-no-deal-brexit.

195 *Events in Iceland Explain Years of Famine in Europe's Dark Ages*, Economist (July 22, 2017), https://www.economist.com/science-and-technology/2017/07/22/events-in-iceland-explain-years-of-famine-in-europes-dark-ages.

195 *After the Deluge: Business and the Effects of Global Warming*, Economist (Feb. 21, 2019), https://www.economist.com/business/2019/02/21/business-and-the-effects-of-global-warming.

Twenty-Five

197 Richard O. Prum, The Evolution of Beauty: How Darwin's Forgotten Theory of Mate Choice Shapes the Animal World—and Us 122 (2017).

197 Caitrin Keiper, *Do Elephants Have Souls?*, 38 New Atlantis (Winter/Spring 2013), 10, 69–70.

198 Adam Gopnik, Paris to the Moon 336 (2000).

198 There are other double moves in the book. One ("even" + "all but") appears in chapter 21: "Ken is a good speaker, <u>even</u> charismatic, as close as you can get to a godless preacher. He has a booming voice, he slaps the palm of his hand to punctuate a point, he <u>all but</u> says amen." A. J. Jacobs, The Year of Living Biblically: One Man's Quest to Follow the Bible as Literally as Possible 98 (2007). Another ("where" + "almost") appears in chapter 22: "<u>Where</u> the L.A. tearoom features birdcage chairs and mirrored daisies, the one in Geneva has an elegant, <u>almost</u> celestial ambience, with tiny starry lights and a fathomless green edging out a darker-than-usual pink as the space's dominant color." Lauren Collins, *India Mahdavi, Virtuosos of Color*, New Yorker (Mar. 12, 2018), https://www.newyorker.com/magazine/2018/03/19/india-mahdavi-virtuoso-of-color.

198 Yascha Mounk, *How a Teen's Death Has Become a Political Weapon*, New Yorker (Jan. 21, 2019) https://www.newyorker.com/magazine/2019/01/28/how-a-teens-death-has-become-a-political-weapon.

NOTES

199   David McCullough, John Adams, 111 (2001).
199   William Golding, Lord of the Flies 141 (Penguin 2003).
199   Jay Winik, 1944: FDR and the Year That Changed History 69 (2015).
199   Mark Twain, *Is He Living or Is He Dead?*, 15 Cosmopolitan 629, 630 (1893).

ACKNOWLEDGMENTS

There are a lot of quotations in this book. Very few of them I tracked down myself. Instead, an amazing collection of law students and undergraduates helped find and catalog the bulk of what you just read. Something that makes their great work even more remarkable: the original cites I gave them were often cryptic and, in some cases, completely wrong. I am very grateful that they are much better at catching my mistakes than I am.

In alphabetical order, the names of these students are Tamar Alexanian, Julia Aust, Rania Baraka, Tony Black, Tyler Berndt, Nick Cagle, Christina Cincilla, Melissa Danzo, Marissa Deardurff, William Derring, Thomas Frashier, Hannah Hoffman, Melody Latino, Patrick Maroun, Jesse Mattox, Marc Mowry, Grace Murra, Kara Naseef, Jose Peralta, Darien Perry, Scotti Petersen, Stephen Rees, Colleen Roberts, Andrea Sinele, Mariah Silverstein, Haley Suggs, Angela Theodoropoulos, Kimiko Varner, Jason Vilaysanh, and Jakin Zhang.

That I was able to include so many students on the project is one of the many reasons I love working with Jason Colman, Amanda Karby, Sean Guynes, and the rest of the team at Michigan Publishing. They think creatively about what success in the world of publishing can look like, and they have been amazingly open to ideas about how to turn the process of producing a book into a teaching opportunity as well. I look forward to starting Volume 2, so we can work together again and get this same double payoff.

www.ingramcontent.com/pod-product-compliance
Lightning Source LLC
LaVergne TN
LVHW051516070426
835507LV00023B/3137